WILLIAM WATTS — A MEMOIR

William Watts
Provost
Trinity College
Dublin

A Memoir

Lilliput/Hinds

Published by The Lilliput Press
62–63 Sitric Road
Dublin 7
Ireland
www.lilliputpress.ie

in association with

Hinds Publishing
13 Carlisle Avenue
Dublin 4
Ireland

First published 2008

ISBN 978-1-84351-141-0

The illustration on the endpapers is taken from a drawing of
The Provost's House by Bee Syms.

Typeset in Garamond
Design by Bill Murphy Design
Printed in Ireland by Betaprint Ltd

To my wife Geraldine (Gerry)

and to my children
Niall, Michael and Sheila,
to whom No. 1 Grafton Street was home

and to
'A College which is singularly incurious about its own history'
– J. P. Mahaffy in his introduction to
The Particular Book of Trinity College Dublin, 1904

CONTENTS

Outside the Walls

Epilogue

Appendices

ILLUSTRATIONS

FOREWORD
by Professor Aidan Clarke

It is a puzzling and faintly disturbing fact that no Provost of Trinity has written a memoir and it is appropriate that Bill Watts should be the one to break the silence. His retirement in 1991 was the unnoticed end of an era. For the previous three hundred years, since the admission of St George Ashe to the office in 1692, the provostship had been held by an unbroken line of twenty-seven Trinity graduates. In many cases, the price of that convention was an unreasonable resistance to change. It was a price that many were only too ready to pay. In other cases, however, the tradition benignly ensured that innovation was sensitive to the ethos and values of the community. It was by slow increments rather than by abrupt lurches that the College evolved into a university without ceasing to be a collegiate body.

I first encountered Watts as a Senior Lecturer endowed with impressively creative pragmatic skills, who bewildered the University Council by the readiness with which he accepted criticism of his proposals and the resilience with which he recast them again and again until they met with the approval of a body which never quite knew when it had crossed the line between discussing the principle and getting the detail right. As Senior Tutor at the time I was particularly impressed with his attitude towards academic appeals. With traditional disdain for natural justice, the Senior Lecturer was present at the meetings of the committee that reviewed his decisions but Watts never attempted to influence the discussion and never questioned the decisions. The characteristics he displayed then foreshadowed a provostship in which determined leadership was combined with flexibility: the aim was unwavering but it was never dogmatic because it amounted to doing what was best for the College within the constraints imposed by differences of opinion. The measure of success was a Board that succeeded in being at once talkative and efficient without deciding a single issue by vote in ten years and a University Council that divided only on appointments to professorships. These were ten difficult years in which growth in student numbers went hand in hand with reduced resources. To the confusion of those who took it for granted that survival and forward planning were the most that could be achieved, Watts insisted on action. To the Treasurer, who dutifully stood guard over the capital reserves, he simply observed: "This is the rainy day that we've been saving for". Financial cut-backs were not allowed to impede development and the 'edifice complex' to which he confesses ensured that the College was well ahead of the game when the financial climate changed in the 1990s.

There are two intertwined themes in these pages. One is the straightforward story of a working class Protestant who made good in both the fundamentally meritocratic hierarchy of Trinity and the impersonally egalitarian world of scholarship. The other is a matter of fact account of what a Provost actually did and the context within which he did it in those rapidly receding days before change ceased to be evolutionary and the College began to lose touch with its past. Both themes reveal interesting contrasts. One evokes a time when the system was sufficiently humane and supple to accommodate a talented student who chose to switch from the arts to the sciences and when strength of character was more important than research funding. The other suggests the fruitfulness of responding to the demands that the new Ireland makes on its universities with a resolute determination to defend the fundamental values of higher education and of Trinity in particular. This has nothing to do with the retention of such quaint survivals as Commons, cobblestones and the conduct of ceremonies in Latin:

it has to do with the preservation of an environment in which scholars can pursue knowledge without constraint and in which students are able to experience that activity at first hand.

This is a story of success, a modern morality tale in which strong principles, common sense and a commitment to public service prevail, but only through the agency of prodigiously hard work. From the foundation of the Central Applications Office to the resolution of the problems of the private hospitals, the memoir quietly records the cutting of a succession of Gordian knots, throwing light into dark corners on the way. And, perhaps most notably and instructively, it reveals how, amidst the plethora of public duties and concerns, Watts found time to continue to indulge the passion for investigating lake-beds for evidence of past climate change that has given him an international reputation in Quaternary Studies. Typically, he pays generous tribute to those who helped him on his way.

In the absence of earlier memoirs we can never know if Watts was the first Provost to clean the lavatories before starting his day's work. I think we may be certain that Gerry was the first Provost's wife to do so. Gently radical and sharply perceptive, Gerry managed to have it both ways. While she continued teaching, made it clear that she was not part of a provostial package and maintained a sceptical distance, she was, nonetheless, always an unobtrusively present source of strength and there was never any doubt that the outstanding success of the Watts provostship was achieved by a team effort.

Aidan Clarke
former Erasmus Smith's Professor of Modern History and
Vice-Provost
Trinity College Dublin

October 2006

ACKNOWLEDGEMENTS

I thank colleagues too numerous to list who have helped me with information and recollections. I was concerned to avoid errors of fact as far as possible. The errors which may appear in the text and the opinions are mine. Nobody else should be called to account for them. I am especially grateful to those who provided me with briefings in writing. Daphne Gill made available the appointments diaries of the Provost's Office which are valuable sources of dates and events. Frank Taaffe of Athy provided information about the old army barracks there. Susan Parkes of the School of Education advised on Model Schools and their staff. Martin Newell checked the details of the foundation of the Central Applications Office (CAO). Ann Sheil of the Provost's Office researched the records on *Educating Rita* and the consequent establishment of the Provost's Fund. Eddie McParland helped me from his rich store of information on the College's buildings and its boundary walls. Eoin O'Neill, Director of Innovation Studies, Salters Sterling, Academic Secretary, Tim Cooper, Director of Buildings, and Mary McGetrick, Information Officer, all assisted me in their own special areas of experience within the College. Brendan Dempsey, College Photographer, helped from his valuable records of people and buildings. Bee Syms is the artist of the pen and ink drawing of the Provost's House used for the end-papers. Micheline Sheehy Skeffington took the excellent photographs of the Burren *Dryas* on page 57. The photo of the ceiling at Fota House is by Fennell Photography courtesy of the Commissioners of Public Works. I am pleased to acknowledge, after all these years, the cartoon by Martyn Turner on my election as Provost. My son Niall helped with computing problems. Help from Ruth Barrington of the Health Research Board, ensured that I had correctly recorded critical dates. Alan Craig of the National Parks and Wildlife Service, at one time a student of mine, kindly read the manuscript and made many helpful suggestions. Tom Raftery of UCC answered questions about Fota, and Herb Wright recalled our scientific research in Minnesota. I thank Ita O'Neill, who typed the manuscript for me.

I have provided a 'further reading' guide at the end of the book in place of a formal bibliography to show where to access the very diverse sources of printed material I have used, from major formal academic studies to pamphlets of limited circulation.

PREFACE

This is the story of how I became Provost of Trinity College Dublin, the road that I followed to get there and my experiences as Provost and afterwards. The story begins with the high point of the election to the Provostship. Then, in 'Prologue' I look back to my childhood in Athy, Co. Kildare, my life as a schoolboy in Dublin and then as a student in Trinity. After graduation I was briefly a member of the academic staff at the University of Hull in Yorkshire, then back to a lecturer's career in Trinity. I became a Fellow in 1960 and Professor of Botany in 1965. 'Ten Years' is an account of my occupancy of the Provostship and of the Provost's House from 1981 to 1991. The Provost lives in 1 Grafton Street, a great Palladian mansion dating from 1761. 'Outside the Walls' tells of my activity outside Trinity, in the Royal Irish Academy, in conservation, in the health services and as Chairman of some unusual charities. Lastly, 'Epilogue' ends the story with my retirement and some reflections on my life and times.

Each Provost necessarily has different kinds of experience to record, each life has its own quality and flavour. I have tried to capture the Trinity of my time as I remember it, as a student, and as a member of the academic staff and Provost. Much of what I have written about the routine of the College is already becoming history for it changes constantly, new procedures are adopted, topics change in importance and the external appearance of a never-changing great institution is a deception. The very life of the College requires constant change, driven partly by necessity, partly by personalities involved in decision-making and their priorities. The sheer growth in student numbers from the 2,000 of my undergraduate days to today's 15,300 brings with it a hard-driving dynamic for change.

No earlier Provost has recorded his life as far as I can determine, most having died in office, and Provosts' wives have been given only a very minor role in history. I have not tried to write a formal history, but have given most space to events and topics that may be of general interest to non-specialists. I did not keep a diary other than an appointments diary but, of course, have access to archival material and to documents which should finally go into the college's records. I have taken trouble to confirm facts and dates and have checked recollections with my friends. Most events in Trinity were in the public domain even before the Freedom of Information Act so that there need be no atmosphere of secrecy. I have tried to be frank without being libellous or hurtful and without invading the privacy of my family and friends. What I can add about Trinity which is personal to myself is my feel of the place and the insider's sense of what was important. This is my own assessment of my life and of my time as Provost from 1981 to 1991; no-one else is to blame for any errors of fact or judgement that may be found.

Provost

The College of the Holy and Undivided Trinity near Dublin

1.
ON BEING ELECTED
PROVOST

IN THE AUTUMN TERM OF
1980 Trinity was surprised to learn that Provost Leland Lyons had
decided to retire from office after the summer term of 1981. He
would then have spent seven years as Head of the College. Ten years
was provided for in the College's Statutes. He had contracted with
Oxford University Press to write a definitive biography of William
Butler Yeats and was finding it difficult to honour his contractual
commitment while much of his time necessarily had to be
dedicated to the many concerns of the Provostship. He was
probably guided in his choice for Yeats by the attractiveness of the
subject with promised access to family papers, and the disciplinary
situation in the College where a series of sit-ins and office invasions
by students, even to placard-bearing students outside his front
door, was making life in College unpleasant.

I was on leave of absence at the University of Washington in
Seattle when the news broke and was surprised to receive a phone-
call from the College Secretary, Gerry Giltrap, to tell me the
astonishing news and to say that it would be timely to consider
whether I wished to compete in the succession stakes. I had
competed unsuccessfully when Leland was elected in 1974 on Dr
A. J. McConnell's retirement. At first I was uncertain whether or
not to stand, for my unsuccessful run in 1974, when I was fifth of
seven candidates, gave no certainty of future success and had left

me feeling rather bruised and unhappy. I asked some of my American friends what they thought and, as true American academics, they advised against, viewing a possible career in administration as a form of desertion to the enemy. When I got home towards the end of the year I had decided to run, impelled by a sort of gut feeling that it was the right thing to do. My wife Gerry said to run if I wanted to, but to remember that failure again was possible. David Webb, my mentor and former Head of the Botany Department also advised against, on the reasonable grounds that the outcome was unpredictable and that unforeseen events could ruin an otherwise good term in office. In spite of the advice I received, I decided to run, but was more realistic about my chances than in 1974 and could face defeat more pragmatically than before.

The election to Provostship in Trinity is a unique procedure. Earlier Provosts had lifetime appointments and, on the death of the incumbent, the Fellows of the College met to elect a successor, usually from among the senior College Officers. Provost Alton who died in 1952 was succeeded by A. J. McConnell, a distinguished mathematician and then Registrar of the College. Dr McConnell saw the period of student unrest in the sixties and seventies which led to a recasting of the College Statutes to provide for modernisation — a ten year Provostship and appointment by an electorate which included all of the College's academic staff with more than one year of service, a small number of administrative staff and some representative students, an electorate of some 380. He had had to deal with difficult issues posed by a proposed merger with University College Dublin (UCD), as did Leland Lyons, but it had already ceased to be an active issue by 1980. Dr McConnell retired on reaching the age of 70, and the new electoral procedure then came into effect. He had seen many changes take place. He was a man of modern outlook who had seen much innovation, much of it supported or promoted by himself. He died in 1998. Candidates for the Provostship were now required to be nominated by a panel of twelve electors. It can be imagined that the election is a rather political process. One needs some keen supporters and a serious policy platform. It occurred to me that, even then, there were members of staff I did not know by sight and quite a few who did not know anything about me, so I produced a CV with my photograph and a statement of objectives. I included a list of my scientific publications to show my academic standing. I don't think Trinity will ever elect a Provost who cannot demonstrate scholarship and a candidate for the Provostship with a business or management background is unlikely to be elected unless he or she has quite exceptional personal qualities with cultural and intellectual interests.

The campaign for the Provostship hotted up in December and was all-consuming during January and until election day in February. Afterwards I recalled that I had made about sixty visits to academic departments to lobby for my cause. On the eve of the election one of my supporters, John Arbuthnott, Professor of Microbiology and subsequently Principal of the University of Strathclyde, asked me about my policies. I replied, 'get as much money together as I can and go like hell'. This was too crude but I was more a pragmatist than a man with a grand vision and thought to seize opportunities as they arose. I was conscious of space and resource problems and decrepit buildings. These would be my early priorities. On the same day it was pouring rain as I walked through the back of the College. I met the College postman pushing his bike with a big satchel of letters. He said, 'I hope you do well for you are a decent man'. It was a good omen.

The election took place in a fevered atmosphere, much enjoyed by everybody but the candidates. A modest book was run on the result. John Healy in *The Irish Times* predicted me as the winner, and jokes were made about white smoke from the Examination Hall. The voting system, the traditional one, is that each elector casts a vote for their preferred candidate by putting a voting slip in a ballot box which is then carried into the adjacent College Secretary's Office for counting by appointed scrutineers. The number of votes cast for each candidate was chalked up on a blackboard and, at each round, the candidate with the lowest vote was eliminated from the count, and eliminated psychologically by having his name rubbed out with a duster. The process is repeated until only two candidates remain. In 1981 five candidates competed. In the first round Máirtín Ó Murchú, the then Senior Lecturer, led with 97 votes, I had 90, then there was a significant gap to 60. Basil Chubb, our Professor of Politics and a distinguished political commentator, came to me and said 'now you've got it'. Those used to elections by proportional representation as he was would have seen that one of the two of us was the likely winner. The others were unlikely to bridge the gap as votes were re-distributed in later rounds. All three were scientists or mathematicians. The majority of their votes came to me and I was elected by 205 votes to 138 (see Appendix 1). The electors adjourned to have lunch and to congratulate or commiserate with the candidates. Gerry and my daughter Sheila had been waiting the outcome in George Dawson's rooms in the Rubrics and we were photographed together, a cheerful group, in Front Square.

In the afternoon I called on Leland and Jennifer Lyons in the Provost's House. We had tea together and exchanged pleasantries. I thought he felt a little depressed by the whole business. The outgoing Provost, after all, would remain in office for some months yet but was already on the way out. He said to me that I was 'a man for the times'. I think he meant, more than anything else, that I would be tough with troublemakers who had caused much disturbance and anger in the College. I'm not sure that I would have coped any better than he had but I had the good fortune that the times were changing, the wave of student protest was receding and only a pale shadow remained when I came into office. I got out of Leland's way for the summer, much of which I spent in the western US at the University of Washington in Seattle. I returned, ready to take up office, at the beginning of September.

New legislation permits the College to elect its own Provost, as was true in the earliest days of the College, but this had been changed by Charles I who was concerned that the choice should be agreeable to him. Until the most recent election which appointed John Hegarty, the names of the first three candidates in order of voting strength had to be sent to the Government for its consideration. It had never been known for it to overrule the

College's choice, but that was technically possible, because our Government had inherited the role of the Privy Council in London in making the appointment. On the evening of the election I received a telephone call at home from the Taoiseach, Charles Haughey. Mr Haughey asked about my schooling. I told him that I was a Dubliner, had gone to secondary school at St Andrew's College and was a citizen of the Republic. He congratulated me and said that my name would be put to the Government on the following Tuesday and that he did not anticipate difficulty. So it transpired. I felt grateful to him for his kindly courtesy on the occasion.

Prologue

David Watts and Margaret Low, grandparents of William Watts, over the fence at Castlemartyr, Co. Cork. They married in 1898.

2.
EARLY DAYS AND ATHY

MY FAMILY

I WAS BORN IN DUBLIN on May 26, 1930, in 7 Upper Mayor Street on the East Wall, the youngest of three children. My maternal grandfather, Thomas Dickinson, was employed by the old LMS (London, Midland and Scottish Railway) to supervise dock workers who loaded and unloaded B and I ships which also carried passengers to and from the railheads at Liverpool and Holyhead in North Wales. Upper Mayor Street was close to the docks, so Grandfather Dickinson could easily walk to and from work, and come home for lunch. The house still stands though threatened by the ever eastwards advance of the Financial Services Centre. My only memory of the house is of lying in bed listening to ships' foghorns on the Liffey on murky winter nights when I was very small, perhaps my earliest memory. The Dickinsons were a Lancashire family, moving by railway postings from Salford to Holyhead and then Dublin. My mother came to Dublin as a little girl, still with some words of Welsh from Holyhead which delighted us.

My Watts grandparents were a mix of Presbyterians from Northern Ireland and from Scotland. My Grandfather David came to Dublin from the Ballynahinch and Clough area of County Down. The Watts family can be traced in the area to a little before 1800, before which I have found no records. Non-conformist Protestants and Catholics alike were not required by law to keep records of births, marriages and deaths until the end of the eighteenth century and few records exist except where rare church records have survived. We had believed that the Watts family were originally immigrants from Scotland, but computer maps of surname distribution show that Watts is overwhelmingly concentrated in Western England around Bath and Glastonbury.

The Watts family may have been farmers but more typically were clergy, teachers, small businessmen and lawyers. One ancestor was a Professor in the Union Theological College in Belfast in the mid-nineteenth century. His portrait still hangs there. Two of my family emigrated to Philadelphia in the 1840s and became shopkeepers, but I have no knowledge of their later lives. I can't claim that they were driven out by famine, more likely they were what we now call economic migrants, driven by too large families and too small resources at home.

My Grandfather, Big Grandpa, to distinguish him from Little Grandpa, my Dickinson grandparent, met and wed Maggie Low, a schoolteacher from Cork, in 1898. Maggie or Meg was the daughter of a Scottish gardener from Stirling who looked after grounds for the Earl of Shannon on his estate at Castlemartyr near Cork. Her mother is commemorated by a headstone in the Church of Ireland cemetery at Castlemartyr, but the Lows dispersed from County Cork, several as emigrants to Australia where they have founded families. The young couple settled in Dublin where my grandfather had come to seek his fortune in various small business enterprises. Unfortunately, after initial prosperity his business failed and, in later life, my grandparents had a very modest income.

One bad effect was that my father William (Will), who was born in 1900, could not be paid for in secondary school, and, with only a primary education, was apprenticed to become a shipyard and engineering workshop worker in Colchester with one of his Low uncles who, in the Scottish tradition, had found careers in shipbuilding and seafaring. Dad was working in the Dublin Dockyard on ship repair in the early 1920s. He once told me 'I brought Collins back from Cork'. This mystified me until I learned that Michael Collins' body was brought by ship from Cork to

Dublin because of the disturbed state of the country at that time. My father was a junior member of the ship's engineering staff. When the Dublin Dockyard closed in the 1920s he was unemployed for a while, then got a job with the Office of Public Works servicing heavy machinery in arterial drainage projects, a job which lasted him until his retirement nearly forty years later. He deeply resented his failure to get secondary or third-level education. His resentment was a major factor in his enthusiasm for better educational opportunities for his children.

Dad was a convinced unionist, believing that breaking the union with Britain was about the worst thing that could have happened. We used to stand for the British National Anthem on the radio but he showed no desire to live in Britain. In fact, like others similarly situated, his experience of being unemployed led to his holding on to his Office of Public Works job like grim death even when other better possibilities offered themselves. He was not well paid. I remember a moment of family ecstasy in the 1940s when his wages rose from £6 to £8 weekly.

As his retirement approached, the fact that he was still officially a temporary civil servant, reappointed intermittently, and therefore non-pensionable, loomed as a huge threat for which his Office of Public of Works superiors produced no remedy. He believed that he was discriminated against on religious grounds, but I think he was more a victim of bureaucratic lethargy and indifference than anything else. He held Denis Purcell, an OPW engineer, in high regard because of his friendliness and support when he felt low. The pension problem was solved in the best 'Irish solution to an Irish problem' manner when my mother lobbied Lionel Booth, a Fianna Fáil TD in our Dun Laoghaire constituency and, fortuitously, a Protestant, who did whatever lobbying was necessary to secure re-classification as a permanent civil servant. My mother, till then a lukewarm Fine Gael voter, reviewed her political allegiance overnight.

Dad's life was lowered in quality by illness. He had rheumatic fever, a disease more easily controlled today, when I was too small to remember, but this may have been the trigger for diabetes. I remember his coming home from work at lunchtime, tossing down two or three glasses of water and falling asleep on a sofa. Now I would recognise this as a symptom of diabetes. He had several periods in hospital for treatment for diabetes and jaundice (hepatitis). The ambulance calling at our house marked each latest crisis. I recall with gratitude the kindness and efficiency of the ambulance crews, usually from the Fire Brigade. Towards the end of his life diabetes reigned and he lost his sight, finally dying grimly in 1965 to a series of brain haemorrhages, which over a short period destroyed his sanity and killed him.

My good memories of Dad are of his best days, a big strong cheerful man helping farmer friends bring in the harvest for steam engines and threshing machines to deal with, letting us ride in hay carts and play in barns. He loved motorbikes and cars. The necessity of his job to visit sites where drainage machinery was at work meant that his car was subsidised so we had car travel when it was still quite uncommon. His hobby was ham radio. He had a private licence and call-sign as EI3P and he constantly built and rebuilt his transmitter, adding new parts and soldering old parts together. He used Morse code in the main, but spoke by voice also. On really exciting days he would receive call-signs from the US and even as far away as Hawaii. He exchanged call-sign cards with others throughout the world. He had good hands, as his job required. He built a caravan which took us on holiday several times and he could make or repair most things. Alas, the genetic inheritance by-passed me. Although my brother, David, became an engineer, I was always clumsy manually, not having the aptitude or inclination to be a good technician.

My mother Bessie or Bess did go to secondary school, the Diocesan School for Girls. It was her extreme steadiness and management of very small resources that kept the family unit going. She helped with our homework so that we could read early and she talked to us about everything that went on in our small society, helping us to understand the adult world. She was altogether dedicated to her family and was willing to face any sacrifice for us. I owe her a deep debt of love and gratitude. I still remember things that moved her. She was shocked in the war years by the loss of great battleships during the Japanese capture of Singapore. She was white-faced at the news of the atomic bombs at Hiroshima and Nagasaki, understanding that this was something new and horrific. We boys saw only a quick victory and an end to the war; my mother told us it was a disaster and a shadow over our whole future. She remained in good health into her 82nd year when she died in Mercer's Hospital after major surgery for a blood clot in her leg.

ATHY

My father's OPW job brought him to Athy, Co. Kildare, the centre from which the arterial drainage scheme for the River Barrow was implemented. His work was the servicing of drainage equipment so our house was full of calendars and pictures of dragline excavators manufactured by Ruston-Bucyrus.

I arrived in Athy within a few days after my birth to join my brother David and sister Bertha. We three children went to the local Protestant national school when we were four years old. The school had started its career in 1852 as a Model School intended to be non-denominational. In 1859 it had 196 Catholic pupils and 121 Protestants. Model Schools had only a brief existence before Archbishop Cullen decided in about 1870 that Catholic children must be in their own church-controlled schools, boys and girls segregated, with the parish priest as school manager. Thus, in practice if not in intention, Model Schools had become Protestant schools within the new state in 1922. By 1934, when I first went to school, older teachers, Mr Rice, the head of the senior school, and Miss Farrer of the junior school had been trained under the old regime and knew little Irish. I remember the day in 1938 when Sammy Atkinson arrived to replace Mr Rice who had retired. He came down the steps into the school yard where we were playing and addressed us in Irish to our baffled astonishment. He was to become one of my most important mentors.

My memories of Athy centre on our experience of family life and the society of its small Protestant community. Protestants in the town, about five families of us with children of the same age, played games together. We met to play rounders and cricket in summer and had parties in one another's houses for birthdays and Christmas. We played traditional games at Halloween like snapping at apples on a string and bobbing to get apples out of buckets by biting. We loved hide and seek games about the barns and sheds attached to several of our houses. At Christmas there were parish parties and games in the Church of Ireland Hall with dipping into bran-tubs and dressing and making up for plays.

The Protestant churches mixed very easily together. There were three of them: Church of Ireland, Presbyterian and Methodist, all three, amazingly, still open. The Presbyterian may be the result of a nineteenth century Duke of Leinster's decision to encourage Scottish immigrants, supposedly especially hard-working and skilled. We went to the Presbyterian Church and Sunday School. In that tradition we learned large chunks of the Bible by heart and much of it has stayed with me. Our knowledge was examined in each year and prizes were given. By a happy mystery we sometimes all got the same mark, thereby eliminating unpleasant competitiveness. Once all four in our class got 99%.

Presbyterians, like Muslims and Jews, respected the Old Testament injunction against images, and churches were very simple, without even the plain crosses which one sees nowadays. My mother, a member of the Church of Ireland, was shocked to discover that Christmas Day was not celebrated though there were traditional carols and readings on the surrounding Sundays. One of the most popular services, for most members were farmers, was the Harvest Festival. The church was decorated with fruits and vegetables, sheaves of wheat tied to the ends of pews, and bunches of flowers, especially Michaelmas daisies. We children were allowed to eat the fruit afterwards. I remember the kindly Mrs Lewis, wife of the Minister, giving us sweet green grapes, the first I ever tasted, and a life-long pleasure.

The town had a weekly market in the Square. Farmers' wives

came with pony and trap to sell eggs and farm-made butter. Not many people had cars then and the difficulties of the war years kept cars off the roads. Fuel was in short supply and Dad made a small business of buying and felling trees for sale as firewood. I got to use the slasher to chop small branches. Locals brought coal fragments from the small colliery at Castlecomer and mixed them with cement to make 'colm' balls (culm is the term for carboniferous strata, mainly shale and limestone with thin coal seams). They glowed splendidly. Later in the war I became an expert at lighting fires with wet turf, which was all that was available at times.

The war didn't make much difference to the way we lived but, of course, there was rationing with food coupons and many shortages. Farmers hated the obligation to cultivate wheat which could be a difficult crop in our wet climate and which made for heavy grey bread. People sang to the tune 'Bless 'em All' 'Bless de Valera and Sean McEntee with the brown bread and the half ounce of tea'. Shortages were greater in Britain than with us, especially in the country. Northerners were worse off for meat and eggs but had good white bread, brought south by visitors when possible. There was a sort of barter economy in those years. Farmers liked really black tea and we had more than enough, so tea was exchanged for sugar so that my mother could make jam. Before the war there was a moment when the harvest of Seville oranges arrived and good housewives made the marmalade supply for the year in one great frenzy of boiling and bottling.

Eggs then were seasonal, so for Christmas cooking they were preserved in water glass (known locally as isinglass) in a great bowl, something now quite unknown and forgotten. There were no bananas during the war. I remember how immediately familiar the taste was when they re-appeared after a gap of years. Our farmer friends, the Moores, made their own butter in a little dairy where the womenfolk turned a big churn, a heavy exercise. The boys of the family coming in from hard physical work in the fields would have a midday meal of potatoes — a bucketful — with a little butter, and plenty of black tea. They caught trout in the river Greese in sacks where there was shallow rippling water and the trout had been frightened out of their deep holes by jumping up and down on the bank. Their grandmother made wonderful soda-bread in flat cakes baked in iron dishes in the ashes of a turf fire. The old lady told ghost stories after dark, made all the more memorable by the distant howling of a dog.

My elder brother David began to cycle all round the countryside to explore old castles. Athy was at the southwest corner of the Pale, controlled by Dublin in the Middle Ages, so there was an array of ruined tower houses which we explored and climbed as far as we could. David introduced me to maps and to curiosity about the countryside and, later, when we were in Dublin, to more ambitious journeys. Once when I was fifteen we biked to Blessington, then through the Wicklow Gap to Laragh near Glendalough, then home by the Sugarloaf, the limit of my endurance, but exhilarating as we came at speed down the Long Hill to Kilmacanogue, a round trip of nearly seventy miles. Once near Athy we came across a lime kiln in use, its floor covered with glowing rock. This, in the war years, must have been about the last use made of lime-kilns. Our range was small, Belan with Shackleton's Mill in ruins, Kilkea with its Fitzgerald Castle and Vicarstown by the towpath along the perch-rich Grand Canal were about our limits. Dad would drive us to Castledermot, famous to us for its five-crossroads where he liked to daydream about cars in the display window of a big garage.

At night in our house we heard the phut-phut of barges on the Grand Canal, invaluable in the war years for transport of big loads like turf or sugar-beet. Some of the barges were still towed by horses and Pack Horse Bridge below the town enabled the horses to cross the Barrow. On summer nights we heard corncrakes calling, now only surviving in a few places, ousted by mechanised agriculture. Our house overlooked the parish priest's (Father Kinnane) thatched house, nevertheless a good house. He kept a big cage for budgies and other small colourful tropical birds. His other hobby was bee-keeping. Once or twice a year his bees swarmed and we rushed to close our windows and watch him go out covered with his net to catch the queen and return her to home.

In 1937 Athy already had electricity but we, separated from the streets by a field, still had oil lamps and we went to bed by candlelight and read by torchlight under the bedclothes. We cooked on a stove with a fire and our radio was driven by an acid battery, a heavy weight which had to be carried to a local chemist for re-charging every now and then. Dad paid £2 to put up a pole in the field and we joined the town's electrical system. It was a great moment.

Apart from his enthusiasm for 'ham' radio he did some shooting with a .22 rifle. He wasn't a very active sportsman but we boys were allowed to creep behind him while he potted at rabbits. Once he shot a wood-pigeon flying over a field. The bird, its eyes glazing over and its feathers blood-spattered, decided for me that I never wanted to shoot. At the outbreak of war, the Gardaí arrived one day and took the rifle, issuing a receipt for it. There was a shortage of firearms for army part-timers, the F.C.A. The rifle never came back and we were paid a small compensation at the end of the war. I have often thought this provided a model for what might have been done at the height of the Northern Ireland troubles. It would undoubtedly have incurred hostility from sportsmen and gunmen alike, many of whom would have retained weapons in secret, but it would have reduced the number of guns in circulation.

We were not very aware of politics but I remember an incident that must have happened early in the thirties. Dad and I were passing through the town square where there was quite a large crowd watching men drilling, but without uniforms or firearms. Dad lifted me up to see and, when I asked what was happening, he said they were Blueshirts, our nearest brush in Ireland with a kind of watered-down fascism. It stuck in my memory because they were just ordinary country boys who were not wearing blue shirts.

The war expressed itself one day in a column of trucks and armoured cars with soldiers passing through the town. It was quite exciting but, even then, I could appreciate that this army would be smashed to pieces in a few brief engagements with a foreign power with modern equipment, in spite of the undoubted courage of the men. Shortly before the war a low-flying small aeroplane appeared once in a while. This was such a novel experience then that we would rush out of the house to see it. It was believed locally to be flown by an army pilot from Baldonnel who would drop letters to his girlfriend as he passed. Certainly we could see him in his cockpit as he came low down.

We did experience some bigotry. Most Protestants kept their heads down but it was easy to feel that we were not seen as really belonging in the country. I've often noticed that well-to-do middle-class Protestants are found to deny that anything unpleasant ever happened, but your position on the social ladder in small rural communities rather determined things; at the bottom you could have unpleasant experiences. Coming home from school a piece of doggerel was often shouted at me 'Protestant dog lepped over the hob ating fish on a Friday'. It is amusing to me that Catholics then regarded eating fish as a penance, while we enjoyed it and still usually have fish on Friday. Once in Belmullet, Co. Mayo, staying at a guesthouse with my boss, Frank Mitchell, the lady of the house, with the acute social perception that Irish people often have without any word being spoken, said, 'You'll be having the fry for breakfast then', and we agreed. In the morning we got our bacon and eggs. Our presumably Catholic fellow-guests suffered on fresh-caught ocean salmon. However, it was frightening for a little boy to be shouted at, with stones occasionally thrown.

I am glad that Bishop Walton Empey, about the same age as myself, remembered similar boyhood experiences in County Carlow, so it was not a unique experience. It is important to record the truth, even if unpalatable by today's standards, but it is also important to record that my other memories of Athy are good and full of the richness of remembered boyhood. One memory of great natural beauty comes back to me. It had been a very cold night and the Barrow must have frozen over briefly in its upper reaches. I stood on the bridge at White's Castle and watched as great discs of ice, a couple of metres across, floated down the river like a fleet under sail.

The house we lived in, 6 Barrow Cottages, was in a former army barracks. The houses were primitive, numbers 1 and 6 had two storeys and were properly serviced; the others were single-storeyed without water or sanitation. Water came from a pump and there were, outside, very inadequate and noisome toilets. I believe the houses were for cavalrymen and their grooms. Our house was very simple, a kitchen, a sitting-room, two bedrooms upstairs and a bathroom with a zinc bath to which we carried hot water on Saturdays, bath-night, and baled out later. The skeleton of the barracks still remained, high walls and pillars and a big iron gate, but it had been unused for a long time and no roofed building remained. We used to explore the grounds looking for bullet-cases which we often found, so there must have been a firing range. I learned that it was last used, briefly, in 1922.

The big gate opened on to a lane which had a farm building and dairy, Costigan's, and a ball-alley. The lane led to Barrack Street at the town end and at the other to a beautiful well where water bubbled up from underground and flowed to the Barrow. The well was walled and had a platform of flagstones around it. I don't think it was ever the site for a pattern or viewed as a holy well, but I remember the beautiful clarity of the water and the frog-spawn in spring at the marshy outflow to the Barrow. The damp meadow around the well was rich in marsh orchids. When the town water supply had one of its frequent crises and water from the taps ran rusty red, we children were packed off to bring back buckets of well water.

I returned to explore Athy with Gerry and my two grandsons in 2002. There were still boys diving into the Barrow from the Packhorse Bridge where the Grand Canal joins the river. The town did not seem very different, but the area in which I grew up is changed utterly. The barracks and Barrow Cottages are completely demolished and the street structure so changed that I could no longer find the lane that led past Costigan's to the well which is now capped. The places of childhood memories have been swept away, brushed from history. In 2003, Frank Taaffe, a local historian, encouraged the Town Council to invite me to Athy to be acknowledged for my achievements and to receive a pewter plate to record the occasion. I had hardly been in the town for sixty years. I was asked who I would like to be present and I said especially the present head of the Model School. On the evening of the presentation I was astonished to find about twenty contemporaries of mine at the school, many of whom I could still remember and recognise. It was a rich occasion. I spoke of the school, my indebtedness to it and my good memories of the town.

Student, Scientist
& Teacher

3.
TEACHERS AND MENTORS

MOST OF US ACKNOWLEDGE the influence and importance of particular people in our lives, especially our teachers. I want to acknowledge some of them here.

I attended national school in Athy from the age of 4. The two teachers belonged to an older generation, Mr Rice (Boss) in the senior school for children over seven and Miss Farrer (Biddy) for the juniors. Miss Farrer was a firm lady given to sudden accesses of fury in which a red colour would creep from her chest up her neck and suffuse her face before receding again, for all the world like the glass-topped petrol pumps of that time which would fill up with a purplish fluid on its way to emptying into the petrol tank. We learned to write on slates and moved on to nibbed pens and inkwells. Miss Farrer slapped us with a pointer when we made mistakes in our tables. She encouraged us to sing and divided us into 'crows' who didn't sing very well and 'canaries' who were a bit better. All of this would horrify teachers today, but she told us about frogs spawning in her garden pond in Dublin and their progress through tadpoles to frogs once more. I remember it very clearly, perhaps she was the first to stimulate my lifelong interest in wildlife.

When I was seven I went to the Adelaide Hospital for an operation for appendicitis. My surgeon was Mr Kinnear whose name-plate was above my bed. I must have been one of Nigel

25

Kinnear's first patients for he must have been in his twenties then with a long life as a surgeon with links with Trinity ahead. The anaesthetic used was chloroform, a soaked cloth held over my nose. In those pre-penicillin days operations were dangerous with possibilities of infection but mine was clean and successful. I spent three weeks in hospital while the wound healed; today three days would be plenty. When I was allowed to get out of bed my legs would not support me and it took a little while to recover my strength. I remember the horrors of hospital food with burnt porridge and tapioca like rubbery frog-spawn but, eventually and after another brief bout in hospital to recover, I returned to normality with energy and strength to get on with life and start back to school.

In 1938 Mr Rice retired and his successor, Samuel Atkinson, arrived. He turned out to be my first important mentor. He taught very well and early on undertook to give me special coaching for an entrance scholarship to one of Dublin's Protestant secondary schools. As it turned out I was eligible for only one school in the state, St Andrew's, the only Presbyterian school. I don't think other Protestant schools would have ruled me out but, formally, there was only one possibility. I remember summer Saturdays sitting in his garden beside the school while we studied the old exam papers that the school provided so that we could assess the standard I would need to reach. I even read biblical history which was on the syllabus. I enjoyed it but had no idea of the standard to be reached. Perhaps a life-long taste for ancient history and archaeology had its roots there. My grandparents' house in Fairview had a huge family bible and an almost equally large Josephus' history of the Jewish Rebellion against the Romans late in the first century AD. The books were dispersed after my grandparents' deaths, much to my present regret. My mother was very anxious at this time, knowing that paying school fees would be very difficult and being quite uncertain about alternatives. I went up to Dublin to sit the entrance examination to St Andrew's, staying with my Watts grandparents, a country boy a bit confused by the big city. One Saturday morning (they still delivered post on Saturdays in those days) a letter came from Mr Southgate, the Headmaster of St Andrew's, to say that I had come first in the examination. The relief was enormous and my fee-free career was settled for the next seven years. That success, for which I acknowledge deep indebtedness to Sammy, was probably the single most important examination in my life. When I became Provost he came to see me one day in the Provost's House. He was retired and living in Dublin. We talked together, he was curious, he said, to see how I was and to give his good wishes for the future. He didn't want to bother me, he said. He left and to my regret I didn't see him again, a modest and retiring man who had done so much.

I enjoyed my seven years in St Andrew's. For the first year, 1941, I lived with my Watts grandparents and travelled by bus from Fairview to the school. Our economies were such that I could save a penny by walking from the school, then at Wellington Place, Clyde Road in Ballsbridge, to the top of Dawson Street outside Geo. Granby's marvellously named 'colonial outfitters' for a single bus ride home on the No. 20. The old house was full of memories of Scottish backgrounds, Scott novels, a print of Robert Burns and a Grandfather clock from Musselburgh dating to early in the nineteenth century which I still have. At the end of my first year my grandmother's health deteriorated. As a result I became a boarder at the school. About 18 months later I was called to the telephone in school. My parents had moved to Dublin and I was to go to their new home in Dun Laoghaire at the end of the school day. I arrived to find my mother happily polishing windows. The house, in Mounttown, though small, was modern and very much better than our Athy home. What had happened was that the OPW drainage operation had come to a halt in the war years. Dad became a storeman to take care of unused equipment, grounded, I think, because of severe fuel shortage during the war. Effectively he had been put in charge of a large lock-up store in Dun Laoghaire. I ceased to be a boarder and a new life began. There was one traumatic aspect. I did not return to Athy for many years. I had been suddenly and decisively cut off from the society in which I grew up.

At school I didn't take to science, defined as chemistry and

27

physics, for biology was not regarded as a subject for boys, only for intending medical students. I was very interested in wildlife and had become a keen birdwatcher, especially of sea and shore birds at Dun Laoghaire's West Pier, but any possibility of taking it as a university subject lay in the future. I will never know whether I could have been good at maths or not, for the school did not then have teachers at a high enough level to prepare pupils for competitive scholarships. I became interested in languages and literature. I read as much as I could lay my hands on of Bernard Shaw and H. G. Wells, both rather neglected writers nowadays, both rich in arguments and ideas, witty and often funny. I probably read as much and as widely in my teens and early twenties as I ever did later.

I was introduced to Ernst Scheyer, my next major mentor. He was a Jewish refugee from Breslau, in eastern Germany, now renamed Wroclaw in Poland, where he had been a judge. He and his family must have got out shortly before the war. He had served in the German army in World War I and would have benefited from the limited mercy Nazis showed to Jewish ex-servicemen. By whatever route, he arrived in Ireland with the support of the local Jewish community. He was allowed to leave Germany with the contents of his 'mappe', an old-fashioned leather briefcase. He carried his war medals and the cap of his student society. I am not sure they would have been my priorities but perhaps they reminded him of times of equality and respect. He spoke little English then and much of that was rather bizarre. Fortunately, Mr Southgate, the Head of St Andrew's, could speak German. I recommend as a method for learning a strange language that you are taught by someone who can barely speak English. There is no option but to speak it and it improves one's pronunciation. Dr Scheyer prepared me for the Trinity College Sizarship examination where my subjects were German and French, the latter taught by his son-in-law, Robert Weil. I also prepared for the Entrance Scholarship which had a wider range of subjects including an English essay and Mathematics.

By autumn I came to accept that I wasn't adequate in maths and was unlikely to win an Entrance Scholarship. I persuaded my anxious parents that I should make a desperate throw of the dice and take whatever risks were involved in pursuing Sizarship alone. Again I came first and my parents were relieved from worries about fees. It is uncertain that I would ever have got to College without Ernst's teaching. My alternatives were a clerkship in an insurance company which was on offer, or to train as a quantity surveyor in the office of a construction company where an aunt was secretary. It amuses me to reflect that in the eyes of the Republic's Catholic majority, Protestants were characteristically seen as well-to-do or just plain wealthy, even perhaps landed gentry: not so in my case or in the case of many others. Sizarship has vanished now, abolished too readily. It was originally for students of limited means who acted as waiters in the Dining Hall. Waiting had disappeared by my time, but there was still a means test. Oliver Goldsmith was a Sizar. It would be good to revive the ancient title for some new category of students from low-income families.

Before I entered Trinity in 1948 my brother David had graduated from Trinity in Engineering and joined the Colonial Service in Kenya, making roads at Makinnon Road. He returned to Britain in 1966 after Kenyan independence. My sister Bertha was already training as a nurse in Liverpool. Neither of them ever returned to Ireland except for rare holidays. It is the typical story of an Irish family in the late forties and fifties.

I began to study French and German for 'mod.' (the honours moderatorship degree in Trinity) with the idea of becoming a secondary school teacher later. I worked hard, enjoyed it, and had good examination results but, probably because of immaturity, did not find my time sufficiently occupied. I began to study law in parallel but did not persist because I found Beuno McKenna's lectures on Justinian and Roman Law very boring and Archie Coutts, a brilliant man, who ultimately became Professor in Bristol, too Tory for me at a time when the tide was turning against Labour in Britain. I favoured Labour and was a keen member of College's Fabian Society.

The Fabian Society, of about fifteen members, was divided about equally between socialists, for whom the Labour Party in Britain was the best model, and the communists, who looked to the Soviet Union, and so may well have attracted the attention of the Special Branch. Senator Owen Sheehy Skeffington was our President. We, the socialist group, rather hero-worshipped him. He was the essential liberal of the fifties, the enemy of all fraud and pretence in argument, especially 'Peace' rallies which seemed to find all virtue on the Soviet side. He was the enemy of authoritarian clerics with whom he battled regularly in the letter pages of *The Irish Times*. Much of that correspondence is recorded in 'The Liberal Ethic' published as a booklet by *The Irish Times* in 1950. I still have a valued copy but the arguments now seem very dated, even extraordinary. Eventually the Fabian Society fell apart, divided irreconcilably between its two parties, and it was swallowed up into the Anti-Apartheid movement, then emerging as a major student concern.

I attended 'Skeff's' lectures in modern French literature which paid special attention to the immediate pre-war years and the intellectual opposition to the rise of Fascism. The lectures were stimulating and combative, the thoughts of a generation that had experienced the Spanish Civil War and Guernica. His lectures on Bernanos were specially memorable. His portrait, by Thomas Ryan, which hangs in the Common Room of Trinity captures him very well. As my student career progressed in my third and fourth years I knew that I wanted a research career. 'Skeff' lectured wonderfully and had a series of research students but published little himself. He would have derided 'publish or perish' but that was the direction to which my mind increasingly turned and I came to admire the dogged comprehensive scholarship of Professor Arnould who published on mediaeval literature and Beaumarchais.

At the end of my second year I won a Foundation Scholarship in French and German. 'Schol' was, and still is, an award for academic performance which freed one from paying fees and gave rights to tenure of rooms in College and free meals on Commons, the College's evening meal. I gladly moved into College rooms which I shared with another old St Andrew's boy, David Caird, as my 'wife', a term liable to be misunderstood today, but it just defined your fellow-tenant. The rooms were on the top floor of number 23 in the Rubrics; now in full cycle I occupy a room at the bottom of number 24. Our rooms had a living-room, bedrooms and a 'skippery' where you cooked to the best of your ability. We had a skip, a male general factotum who kept the place clean and decent. Skips are no more, now replaced by women cleaners.

Again I felt underemployed. I had a general interest in geology, acquired from my brother, and in field biology, especially bird watching, a passion I still enjoy. I thought I would enjoy a more disciplined knowledge of the natural sciences. I saw it more as a hobby than as a potential career. I asked the college for permission to study for two degrees and was allowed to proceed, subject to the wishes of the necessary three departments concerned. My tutor, J. D. Smyth in Zoology, a parasitologist with a good research record, heard my story, told me he didn't mind personally, that I did not have sufficient background to study Zoology, but if others would accept me, so be it. I don't contest that judgement; I was lucky to be accepted by others. I was accepted by botany, geology and geography and this laid the foundations of my subsequent academic life.

I encountered two very remarkable mentors: David Webb, Professor of Botany and Frank Mitchell in Geology. Both men played very important roles in my career and influenced me greatly. David had an exceptionally fine intellect, perhaps the most brilliant I met in College. He was occasionally cranky, snobbish and difficult, and a slightly terrifying figure. Apart from Botany he had very wide interests and knowledge. He wrote a fine history of the College's academic development from its foundation in joint authorship with R. B. McDowell. He was a fine stylist in English and his contribution shines through the book. He also had a deep understanding of the College's Statutes and devoted energy to revising them. His subject, plant taxonomy, the naming and description of plants, requires exacting judgement. He deplored what he saw as ever increasing inaccuracy and carelessness in the use of English. I remember his lectures very well and, above all, the field trips he led, usually to Kerry to study the native flora and, on one memorable trip, to the Rhine Valley and the Black Forest. He was widely travelled, especially to Spain and Portugal, but even as far as Madagascar, about which he gave a memorable lecture. He and Frank Mitchell both made me aware that our subjects made many opportunities to travel outside Ireland and to be free from a purely national focus. I came to recognise David's considerable international standing as a scientist and his many contacts. I began to form a clear sense of what research was and I knew I wanted to pursue it. He was very helpful to me subsequently as I shall relate.

Frank Mitchell was ultimately my most important mentor and a personal friend. He combined high academic achievement, practical administrative ability and a capacity to move easily in Irish society. He became a Fellow of the Royal Society of London in 1973 and President of the Royal Irish Academy in 1976. He taught Quaternary Geology, essentially the geological and climatic record of the Ice Age and the recent period. The Ice Age occupied the last two million years or so, but Frank's interest focussed on the last 15,000 years. He also taught Irish archaeology, not then or now formally provided for in Trinity, in a very successful voluntary late afternoon course remembered by many. The Ice Age is a complicated period of advances and retreats of ice-sheets, ice-free cold periods, and interglacial periods with climates as warm as at present. Then bogs grew and lakes laid down deposits just as they do now. In the cold periods these peat and lake muds were largely destroyed when overrun by ice, but some survived. They contain fossil plants, some of which no longer occur in Ireland and they can be studied by the fossil pollen, seeds and fruits they contain.

Frank described how his friend Tony Farrington, Secretary to the Royal Irish Academy and a distinguished field geologist, returned to the Academy having discovered an interglacial lake deposit buried by boulder-clay, exposed in a stream section near Gort in Co. Galway. Knud Jessen, Frank's Danish mentor and famous for studies of interglacial floras in Denmark, had not found any Irish interglacials and had promised a beer to anyone who found one. Farrington produced two cones of silver fir from the Gort deposit, not yet disintegrated, which happens as the seeds ripen. Silver Fir is commonly planted today but is not now a native tree. For this, Jessen exclaimed, two beers, a good promise from one who was also a director of the Carlsberg Foundation. Frank told this story and told of a new interglacial deposit found during digging a shaft for a well at Kilbeg, County Waterford. So far there had only been a preliminary study. This seized my imagination. I desperately wanted to study it. It had a feeling of buried treasure like a major archaeological find. When I returned to Trinity in 1955 Kilbeg became my major task which led to visits to Jessen in Copenhagen.

Like David Webb, Frank was a formidable traveller, He travelled to the US to visit the Mid-West and California just after the war when travel by boat and train was still normal. Both men were generous hosts and also generous in the trouble they took to introduce me to leading scientists. I learned a lot from them about how to enthuse and support graduate students.

David died in 1994 in a car accident. He was 82 years old. He is commemorated by a plaque above the small graveyard behind the College Chapel. Frank's death at 85 took place after a short illness in 1997. Frank had asked that there not be a formal religious ceremony when he died. It fell to me, in consultation with his daughters, Lucy and Rosamond, who were living outside Ireland, to organise a celebration of his life and achievements. This took place in the Edmund Burke theatre in the Arts Building some months later. The several hundred people who crammed this large lecture theatre to overflowing were a tribute to the breadth of his contacts and his popularity within Irish society and the academic community. Members of his family, former graduate students, friends and neighbours from Townley Hall spoke in his memory. We saw him on film. It was a unique and memorable event.

At the end of my undergraduate career in 1953 I held two degrees but even then saw the Modern Languages option, especially German, as my career. I spoke to Professor M. F. Liddell, 'Maxie', a kindly and much-liked man, about the possibilities of research in Trinity. He thought that Trinity would not be a good option, but offered to introduce me to colleagues in Oxford. I was not able to consider this for financial reasons and my imagination was not then able to make the jump I would need to support a move to another university. I went to David Webb and asked him if he would supervise me for a doctoral thesis in plant ecology. He said yes unhesitatingly and thus made my career choice for me.

Finally I should mention my American mentor, Herb Wright, Professor at the University of Minnesota, about whom I also write in a subsequent chapter. He was a very large influence in my life, teaching me field and laboratory skills and introducing me to the American scale of doing things and the possibilities it opened up. About half of my research life and publication has been US-based and half in Ireland and continental Europe. Herb also taught me a great deal about scientific writing and the preparation of papers for publication. With time my research took me from Minnesota to elsewhere in North America, especially Florida and the Southeast, but also to the Pacific Northwest and to the highlands and tropical lowlands of Mexico. Herb was Head of the Limnological Research Center (LRC) at the University of Minnesota. Now ninety, he is the grand old man of North American Quaternary Studies. I had study periods at the LRC over several years in the 1960s and 70s. Since then most of my American friends and colleagues in various centres have been LRC graduates, held together by a network of common experience in a remarkable lab headed by a remarkable man.

4.
TRINITY AS I SAW IT

I ENTERED AS AN UNDER-graduate in 1948 and left in 1953 to return from England two years later. The old Trinity was changing. Top hats and morning suits at the College Races and strawberries and cream at the Elizabethan Garden Party were receding into the past. In the war years the College had kept going as well as it could, but some of the staff and the students went to Britain for war service and shortages had been a problem. There were air-raid shelters in College Green and water tanks for fires. Frank Mitchell organised patrols for the Old Library roof to extinguish incendiaries. Fortunately nothing happened, although a German bombing of the North Strand in 1941 with 34 deaths and the destruction of houses, was a reminder of what could happen rather casually in wartime, because bombers returning from a raid on Belfast dumped their remaining bombs.

When I entered as a Junior Freshman (first-year student) we still had three seven-week terms separated by seven-week vacations and a slumberous Long Vacation in summer. There were examinations every term and a general examination in six subjects called Littlego which could be taken in every term but had to be completed with passing grades by the middle of the Junior Sophister (third) year. To pass, a mark of only 3 out of a maximum of 10 was required. It still came close to being my undoing. Languages were not a problem but my mathematical weakness was cruelly exposed and I just

35

scraped it with an ability to calculate the mysteries of ships passing lighthouses, the velocity of discharged bullets and the principle of moments. Logic, which I have never really understood as learned from Abbott's *The Elements of Logic*, was also a weakness. Instructed to 'Construct Barbara' by an irascible Church of Ireland cleric, I made a mess of it. I did not enjoy 'Not much of a scholar are you?'. The examination was a fearsome hurdle for many, including myself, and I did not regret its demise some years later, but the idea of a general examination testing ability in English, other languages and mathematics now including computing, has much to commend it in principle.

The examination had one feature surviving from older forms of instruction, an oral examination. Regent's House, the large room over Front Gate, was filled with students on examination days writing answer papers and interrupted by being called for *vivas* held in the same room in a huddle with one of the many examiners present. Bedell Stanford, our Professor of Greek, and subsequently Chancellor, was lying dying of cancer when he told me he had a confession to make. 'I cheated at Littlego!' he confided. As a student of Classics the Latin examination was very easy for him and was completed within ten of the allotted thirty minutes. On either side were strugglers. He wrote an answer with a few deliberate mistakes for each of them and passed them undetected to either side. I said I thought it could probably be forgiven now, though he had a sense of humour and had enjoyed it all. Owen Sheehy-Skeffington told a good story of Sir Robert Tate struggling in a *viva* with a weak candidate, a rugby player and therefore favoured. He exploded 'Oh my God, you are an ass, I can only give you three!'.

In those days everyone wore gowns and, especially in Arts, one would be expelled from lectures if arriving gownless. Gowns were disappearing in Science. They were not required in practicals and, soon after, lost out in lectures too. The undergraduate gown still survives in the Choral Society and Chapel Choir. Scholars of the House moved on to grander gowns with long flowing sleeves. They could be paid £10 annually as 'waiters' who declaim the Latin grace before and after the evening meal known as Commons. The grace had to be said *memoriter* (from memory), without any recourse to reminders, from a wooden pulpit shaped like a classical bowl. The first performance was a considerable ordeal but one soon remembered it without difficulty. I still remember it and have said it many times. One or two 'waiters' never overcame the *memoriter* ordeal and dropped out. An added distraction was R. M. Gwynn (Old Daddy) who would shuffle up to the pulpit, produce his brass ear trumpet and raise it to the speaker. It made strange squeaks, surely already an out-of-date technology in the fifties.

At Commons ties were compulsory. Tom, the Postman, who knew everyone's name, kept a Roll of Attendance and rolled back polo-necked sweaters to make sure there was a tie beneath. It was his duty to call out 'Stand, Gentlemen, for the Provost', when he attended. Commons was then obligatory for students in residence. This resulted in a full Dining Hall for two sessions every evening. The Fellows processed to High Table. They walked and sat at table in order of seniority by date of election. A great deal of manoeuvring and shuffling took place to make sure that each Fellow processed in the right order on entering and on leaving to take coffee upstairs in the Common Room. Coffee was poured by the youngest member present. Members of the academic staff who were not Fellows came last in the procession. I remember Professor Liddell, who was not a Fellow, engaging in elaborate footwork to keep in step with his companions whom he called, without a trace of irony, the Olympians. All this is gone now. There is no procession in the old sense. Commons has ceased to be compulsory and is poorly attended, sustained by a few resident Fellows and the Scholars.

It is worth saying that the institution of Scholarship is very valuable. It dates from the very beginning of the College. Elections to Fellowship and Scholarship take place on Trinity Monday. The Scholars form a corps of students chosen by examination for their academic distinction who, without undue emphasis, form an elite among the undergraduates. Free Commons and access to residence are among their privileges. Scholars are invited to revisit the College for the Trinity Monday dinner on each tenth anniversary of their election. Scholars of the Decades meet old friends again and meet with Scholars of other decades. I became a Scholar in 1950. The Trinity Monday dinner of 2000 which I attended was also attended by a Scholar of 1930. An eighty-year old scholar elected in 1890 could have attended my Trinity Monday dinner in 1950. I hope to last at least until 2010 myself. We Scholars represent a collective memory spanning more than a century, a group with special obligations of loyalty to the College and its traditions.

First-year students in rooms attended night roll to ensure that they were present in College as regulations required. The Junior Dean, a Fellow with responsibility for undergraduate discipline, walked, capped and gowned, to night-roll in the lobby of the Dining Hall, preceded by a porter carrying a lantern. I remember Dr Pyle on one such occasion on a murky winter's night, lighted by the lantern, a very memorable scene, worthy of an artist. Many people think that Trinity's impressive walls and railings, begun in Nassau Street in 1842 (the creation of John and Robert Mallet of Dublin, engineers and ironfounders) were intended to distance the College from ordinary citizens and keep them out. Not so, the night-roll shows that the College's objective was to keep students in, and under some modest discipline. Even the earliest records from the College's first century document expulsions or punishments for riotous behaviour and consorting with unsuitable women.

Night-roll has now disappeared, student discontent in the 1970s and 80s had led to the slackening or abolition of many old practices. The title 'Regius' for professorial appointments which would have required the approval of the Privy Council in London in the past, lapsed because it had ceased to have any legal meaning. V. M. Synge, Professor of Medicine and Consultant at Baggot Street Hospital was the last known to me to be addressed simply as 'Regius'. Attendance at Chapel was obligatory and recorded by 'markers' for members of the Church of Ireland. It was unenforceable and later abandoned while institutions such as the Gentlemen of the Choir who sang at morning service disappeared under financial stringency. Provost Alton who died in 1952 had a butler, Smeaton. His successor Provost McConnell no longer had a butler, but had a Lady Housekeeper. All of these posts were unsustainable and the Provost's House today survives with a small staff of no great pretension.

Women students, although steadily increasing in number in the 1950s, were far from being fully accepted. They could not be in College after 6 p.m. except to walk from Front Gate to the Library, signing on and off in both places. Women were not admitted to the Common Room or Dining Hall so women academic staff and students alike were confined to the cramped premises and dining facilities of House No. 6. Ultimately in 1968, women were admitted to Fellowship and Scholarship. Earlier, admission to the Common Room in 1958 had taken two ballots, both presided over by Professor Donald Wormell, a liberal and forward-looking Senior Lecturer. The first vote was for the status quo by a small majority, older, and even some younger men, imagining endless gossip, overheard conversations and so on, none of which looks very realistic today. The second vote was for change. I was present on both occasions and voted twice for change. One huge benefit of women becoming Scholars with Scholars' rights of residence was a great improvement in the quality of College rooms, especially showers and decent toilet facilities. When I was a resident from 1950 to 1952 there was a tap and sink outside our rooms and chamber pots for the unfortunate skips, male servants, to empty, an unimaginable scene today.

It is hard now to realise how far Trinity had been excluded from Irish life. The hostility of the Roman Catholic Church, especially shown by John Charles McQuaid as Archbishop of Dublin, meant that few Catholic students were present and they were mostly from outside Ireland or outside the Dublin diocese. The Protestant population was small, too small to sustain a university, but the College was enriched by the aftermath of World War II: British ex-servicemen, some British school-leavers, often with family connections with Ireland, Nigerians and other colonials soon to achieve independence, and many others; students from Northern Ireland were specially significant. Older Trinity graduates speak with nostalgia of the diversity and international character of the student body at that time. The British presence meant that, when George VI died in 1952 and Elizabeth was proclaimed to be monarch, British students stood up at the end of Commons and sang 'God Save the Queen'. I was there and was taken totally by surprise. I see it now as a last expression of a dying past from which Trinity had to move on.

5.
DEPARTMENT OF BOTANY

I GRADUATED IN 1953 WITH first-class honours in Natural Sciences (Botany with subsidiary Geology). I had earlier (1952) gained a first in Modern Languages (German and French) with higher marks than in science. Marks were published in full, down to decimal points, in those days. Nobody would try to overlap two degrees nowadays and probably would not receive permission if it was proposed, rightly in my view. It is both stressful and does not allow the candidate to pursue either subject in sufficient depth.

I had become committed to a career of research in plant ecology, and especially in Frank Mitchell's subject, Quaternary palaeoecology, the history of the vegetation cover of our landscape in the last 2 million years or so. I applied for a junior lectureship in Botany at University College, Hull, then a college of London University which became independent as the University of Hull with its own charter in 1954. There was little competition, three candidates, for there was a general shortage of potential university staff in the immediate post-war years, and I won the appointment. This was not a good career move. Nobody would now appoint a just-qualified undergraduate to a teaching post. My training and depth of knowledge were simply insufficient for the job to be discharged. I survived but often only just ahead of the rather mature group of would-be secondary school teachers I would face in class.

With my experience with David Webb, I introduced field work with trips to see the vegetation of the chalk hills of the Yorkshire Wolds and a memorable field trip to Corfe Castle in Dorset at the edge of heath and peatland around Poole Harbour which had a rich and rare flora. An introduction at Hull to the possibilities of field work was probably my main contribution which would be valuable to teachers. I also enjoyed contributing to the development of Hull's Botanic Garden. My Head of Department, Professor Ronald Good, author of a well-received textbook on plant geography and an experienced plant taxonomist, looked benevolently on my interests.

Gerry had preceded me to Hull as a supply teacher to a secondary modern school for the Local Education Authority. It was chance that brought us to the same city. We had expected to have to find jobs in different cities in Britain, for Ireland had few opportunities to offer in those days. We married in 1954 at a ceremony in the local Registry Office, called Ernest Bevin House, for Hull was a Labour stronghold. The Registrar reminded us of the solemnity and seriousness of the occasion, a thought that required Gerry to suppress a giggle. It would be nice to be able to assure that decent, serious, dark-suited man that we are still together fifty years later.

Hull ended for me because those were the days of compulsory military service, liability for which ceased after the age of twenty-six, but after two years residence I was liable and not yet twenty-six. I was summoned to join the Army and after a brief discussion with the recruitment officer had to recognise that this could not be avoided. I resigned my post and we returned to Dublin. I had and have no hostility to the British Army; I just didn't wish to serve in any army. I am grateful to that Army for determining my future for me. Without that decision I would never have had the opportunities that opened up for me in Trinity. In retrospect the Hull experience was a false start. I was not mature enough or sufficiently trained for the job I undertook. I lacked the experience of working for a doctorate, which would be normal today as a foundation for an academic career, and I had not followed up on my first intention to register for a Trinity PhD with David Webb.

My return to Dublin with possibilities for real research was very welcome to me.

Looking back to our time in Hull, there are good memories. We went to concerts by the Yorkshire Symphony Orchestra in the Town Hall, voted in a general election and heard a fiery speech by Aneurin Bevan who put down hecklers with ferocity. 'I see you wear a beard to hide your weak mouth', he cried, for few men wore beards at that time. We enjoyed visits to historic towns, York, Beverley and Lincoln, and experienced Dickensian fogs in winter, dense and sulphurously smelly. Bus conductors walked in front of their crawling vehicles. One felt one's way along walls and peered to read street names. Hull was in the 'tripe belt' and whole shops existed to sell tripe, sheep's reeds and other unimaginable bits of animals' digestive systems. We liked to visit the market. Hull was still a great fishing port before the 'Cod Wars' with Iceland. All kinds of fish were for sale and, especially, large edible crabs which we enjoyed. In autumn wild mushrooms, 'blewitts', never sold in Ireland, were on the stalls. I watched soccer and rugby league matches. I still look at the papers every week to follow Hull City's progress, currently good after some dismal seasons, a final ghost of those early years.

On my return to Dublin Frank Mitchell gave me a job as a Research Assistant. Gerry obtained a teaching post in the Diocesan School for Girls where my mother had been a pupil many years before. An odd thing happened. The third member of the Botany Department, Derrick Boatman, was Assistant to the Professor, a position that had very little promise of promotion. The 'assistant' category no longer exists. Derrick was understandably discontented. He applied successfully for the job I had vacated which was now advertised. A few months later David Webb offered me the empty Junior Lecturer's post in Trinity. Effectively, Derrick Boatman and I had swapped posts. Posts in Trinity could be filled very informally in those days by procedures which would be unacceptable today.

As my academic career developed I published some research papers in the *Proceedings of the Royal Irish Academy*, became a full lecturer, was appointed to a Fellowship in 1960 and became a member of the Academy in 1964. When I first became a Junior Lecturer I was paid £400 a year, quarterly, in arrears. Becoming a Fellow brought my salary to £1000, now paid monthly, a liveable amount in those days, princely in comparison with what had gone before. Becoming a Fellow then brought a raise in salary; today it is an honour and recognition of achievement without a financial reward.

In 1965 I became Professor of Botany. David Webb had come to me one day and said that he had been Professor for fifteen years but he had run out of ideas as a Departmental Head and would like to devote his time to research. He was deeply involved in the production of *Flora Europaea*, a five-volume comprehensive flora of Europe, the first such ever produced, and a major academic achievement. He was on its editorial committee. He proposed that I should take over as Professor, provided he retained a second professorial chair and salary. I was naturally excited at the suggestion, which David then took through whatever processes were necessary by the Board. Everything fell into place without controversy. It couldn't happen today. I honoured David's example in 1980 when I retired as Professor of Botany after fifteen years. I applied for and was appointed to a personal chair in Palaeoecology, vacant because of Frank Mitchell's retirement. A year later I was elected to the Provostship. For that post, at least, I competed successfully before a critical electorate.

In 1955 Botany was a department of three, David Webb as Professor, George Dawson, recently a graduate student in Cambridge and a missionary for genetics, and I. We did our best to cover the whole subject but it was a nearly impossible task for only three people. Over the years the numbers of staff rose to seven and it was more possible to teach one's own specialism as well as cover more basic topics such as the morphology of major plant groups, which any of us could cover at a simple level. In due course, George Dawson departed to found the Department of Genetics.

David's work on *Flora Europaea* had led to a focus on the herbarium, an important collection of dried plants with major collections dating from the mid nineteenth century. Professor W. H. Harvey had collected in South Africa and published *Flora Capensis*. He also collected algae (seaweeds) from the southern oceans, especially the Pacific. There are numerous type specimens (first description of a new species from a preserved specimen) on which plant nomenclature is based. If this may seem dusty and old-fashioned it is the basis for a precise description of plants and vegetation, essential to modern conservation.

The Department at present is studying the Flora of Thailand under John Parnell's direction. Several of our graduate students have gone on to distinguished appointments in centres of plant taxonomy such as Kew and Glasnevin. The Department has joint teaching programmes with Environmental Science. Prof. Mike Jones has led research into the cultivation of *Miscanthus* (Elephant Grass) as a biofuel. This work was much reported from the British Association meeting in Dublin in 2005. Ireland's very extensive commitment to reducing CO_2 emissions as part of the Kyoto protocols makes it necessary to explore such alternative energy sources. The Department has been strong in research and has had good success with research funding and in numbers of graduate students.

My own involvement with College's central administration led to several periods of absence from the Department during which David Jeffrey, an ecologist and conservationist, stood in for me. I owe him a great debt of gratitude and apology for placing administrative burdens on him. He also continued a conservationist programme in An Taisce, the National Trust for Ireland, where he played an important leadership role and became President.

The Department has long managed a Botanic Gardens. Starting in 1687 after several false starts as a Physic Garden (with plants of value in medical practice) a definitive start was made in 1806 when 8 acres were leased from the Pembroke Estate at Lansdowne Road. The lease was for 175 years. Later a further 3½ acres were added and the Gardens enclosed by high iron railings much of which still survives. In 1960 the College, over opposition from the botanists, sold a large part of the site of the Gardens to allow the construction of the Intercontinental (later Jury's) Hotel. The remainder of the old Gardens was sold to become the Berkeley Court Hotel in the late 1960s. It was regrettable. The site had enormous potential value, very large indeed at today's values but the lease was nearing its end and the College's then powers-that-be decided to sell.

I had become Professor by then. The transfer of the Gardens to Trinity Hall in Dartry was negotiated and carried out in 1966–67. I had a large measure of responsibility for the plan and the design of the new Gardens which included new greenhouses, a laboratory and some controlled environment rooms. Many plants, even small to medium-sized trees, were dug up and transferred from the old Gardens, a mammoth task. Gratitude must be expressed to the Head Gardener, Denis McKennedy and his team for quite exceptional loyalty and effort at a difficult time. Very few plants were lost in the transfer and new initiatives became possible with the keeping of rare species for conservation purposes and of native Irish plants of wild origin. The Gardens have survived a programme of new building at Trinity Hall and will, I trust, continue to survive, even if still apt to attract the attention of cost-cutters.

I still visit the Department frequently and am delighted by its continuing success, especially its attractiveness to graduate students.

The Provost in Library Square in 1988.
Photo Digital

Above: Election Day, 1981. Gerry, Sheila and the newly-elected Provost meet in Front Square after the result was declared.

Below: Cartoon by Martyn Turner from the Trinity College Gazette, the University of Dublin Staff Journal, Friday 13th March 1981.

Portrait of the Provost by Derek Hill, painted at the artist's home near Churchhill, Donegal, 1988.

Saloon of the House.

Above: *David Webb presents his portrait to the Provost for the College collection.*

Below: *David Webb, after a portrait by Andrew Festing, 1983 which wittily displays his love of saxifrages and of wine.*

Frank Mitchell, after a portrait by David Hone, 1985, in the College collection.

William Watts — a Memoir

Above: *Crown Prince Akihito of Japan, with Crown Princess Michiko and the Provost in the Provost's House.*

Below: *Chancellor Frank O'Reilly, King Juan Carlos of Spain and the Provost waiting for the Commencements Procession.*

Above: *Alexander Dubček, Czechoslovak statesman at Commencements on 12 July 1991 with Daphne Gill, Secretary to the Provost.*

Below: *Professor Dermot Hourihane, Chairman of Trinity Week, President Hillery, Gerry, the Provost and Máire Hourihane.*

The Dining Hall after the fire of July 1984.

The Dining Hall after restoration, 1985.

Above: *Sir Anthony O'Reilly and the Provost, in conversation in the Drawing Room.*

Below: *Lady Normanby, Pro-Chancellor and benefactor of the College, discussing Cook voyage artefacts with Dr Michael Ryan of the National Museum.*

Above: *Winter coring from thick ice at Elk Lake, Minnesota.*

Below: *Core with late glacial sediments from a Burren lake.*

The core below shows, in a short length, changes over 3,000 years. At the far right, a sticky blue-grey clay records the melting of ice of the Last Glaciation. The white marl to the left of this marks a warm period, followed by a grey marl of a regression to a cooler climate. The next white marl marks the period of grassland when giant deer flourished. Then a thin black silty clay marks the Younger Dryas period, a severe climatic deterioration when the giant deer became extinct. The last white marl at the left is of the Post-Glacial when the landscape became covered by forest.

Above: *Herb Wright and Cathy Whitlock with a surface mud-core in a perspex tube, taken from a small lake in Yellowstone National Park c. 1985*

Below: Dryas octopetala *in the Burren, flowers and distinctive leaves.*

Above: *The Provost robed as President of the Royal Irish Academy after his retirement as Provost.*

Below: *The Provost being introduced to Pope John Paul II by the President of the Pontifical Academy of Science.*

Above: *With Davis Coakley, Professor of Medical Gerontology at St James's Hospital on the occasion of the announcement of the Watts Clinical Research Fellowship in Geriatric Medicine.*

Below: *Brian Weir, Headmaster of St Patrick's Cathedral Grammar School, Dean Griffin and the Provost at the laying of the commemorative stone for the new Grammar School in 1983.*

Above: *Three Provosts* (l. to r.)*: John Hegarty.
2001– ; Thomas Mitchell, 1991–2001; William
Watts, 1981–1991.*

Below: *Gerry entertains President Chaim Herzog
of Israel in the House.*

Above: *Fota House, Contract signing for restoration, left to right seated: Aidan O'Shea Contractor, W. W.; standing: Prof. Tom Raftery, John Cahill Senior Architect OPW and Gabriel Gleeson Assistant Principal Officer OPW.*

Below: *Fota House, the restored roof in the drawing-room.*

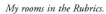

SAMUEL BECKETT

9308/511

Paris
23.4.86

Dear Dr Watts
Thank you for your letter
of April 17.
I accept with pleasure
and gratitude the honour
you propose.
With best wishes for the Centre,
I am
yours sincerely
samuel Beckett

Samuel Beckett's card giving permission to name the Samuel Beckett Theatre in his honour.

My rooms in the Rubrics.

62

6.
RESEARCH: POLLEN AND CLIMATE

INTRODUCTION

IN THIS CHAPTER I FIRST try to give a broad perspective of research as it developed into the modern age in Trinity and how my research career began. Research has developed in complexity throughout my lifetime, particularly in the last twenty years. Explaining the underlying technologies, especially in securing reliable and exact chronologies, is beyond the scope and ambition of this book, so I try to give some pointers to them in the bibliography. After my introductory account I describe three research projects to give a flavour of the work I have been involved in as a sole author or, increasingly, with others in research teams. The first looks at Ireland, while the second and third, in Italy and the United States, are in the mainstream of modern Quaternary studies and climatology.

SCIENTIFIC RESEARCH IN TRINITY

In Trinity modern concepts of experimental laboratory-based scientific research in well-equipped buildings were strongly advocated by G. F. Fitzgerald, Professor of Physics. Fitzgerald, the importance of whose publications was given recognition by election to Fellowship of the Royal Society, declared that it was the duty of universities to carry out research. He led a campaign to enlarge education in the sciences by obtaining funding for new buildings for Physics (1905) and Botany (1907). On his death in 1901, his campaign was brought to completion by John Joly, Professor of Geology, a distinguished and original researcher in his own right. He too was a Fellow of the Royal Society. E. T. S. Walton's career in physics, culminating in a Nobel Prize in 1951, added enormous distinction to the Department of Physics when it was still struggling with inadequate resources. The idea that Fellowship in College should be linked to research was finally affirmed in 1944, when the Board found itself short of suitable candidates and unable to conduct interviews or place advertisements usefully because of wartime conditions. It was decided to advertise two fellowships internally without restriction of subject. Twelve lecturers applied and their CVs and publications were laid on a table outside the Boardroom. Webb and McDowell tell of a Senior Fellow, 'to whom a reprint from a learned journal was an unfamiliar object', who was heard to refer to the candidates as 'those bloody pamphleteers'. Frank Mitchell, my mentor, and Gordon Quin, a distinguished scholar in Old Irish, were the two 'pamphleteers' selected.

This event marked the approaching end of the era in which fellowships were advertised by subject which was dictated by teaching needs. They were competed for by taking a gruelling examination and a *viva voce* before assessors. This was followed by a lecture before the Board in the Examination Hall. The process was known as the 'prelection'. Subsequently, the concept that the primary duty of Fellows was to administer the College, to teach and to have scholarly competence in their subject, has given way progressively to evaluation by published work. The system is now thoroughly bureaucratic with provision for external assessment of publications. 'Publish or perish' is too extreme a characterisation of the challenges facing young lecturers today but promotion is tightly linked to a good publication record.

To a young scientist like myself in the fifties and sixties the sending of reprints to leading researchers in one's field throughout the world was a source of much pride and satisfaction. The practice is now obsolescent with more and better international journals and easy access to them by computer. Now one's standing in research is assessed objectively by citation indices which record how often one's publications have been referred to in the bibliographies of articles in major journals. In other words, has anybody read your work and found it worth citing as a source of information and how many have done so (see Appendix 2 on my own work). A surprising number of articles are cited only a little or not at all. The citation index method is imperfect because it cannot adequately take account of book chapters, occasional publications not in journal form, multiple authorship or conference abstracts. It also gives some encouragement to repetitive publication of essentially the same information. Nevertheless, it gives a reasonable approach to assessing a scientist's standing with his peers and its methodology is constantly being improved.

From the seventies there was a steady growth in research publication in all subjects but perhaps especially in the Sciences and Medicine, where a high productivity in shorter papers for journals is characteristic. A quick comparison of numbers of publications listed in the College Calendar for 1960 and 1990 shows a more than tenfold increase in that time. A great increase in the number of candidates preparing for doctoral or masters' theses has established a research culture. The single scholar working and publishing alone would have been a true characterisation of the work of Frank Mitchell and David Webb, although David was a co-editor of *Flora Europaea* with five others. More recently, research is increasingly carried out by teams of established scientists and graduate students with publication in multiple authorship, each member bringing a particular specialised skill or personal contribution to the group, so that it is often not possible to identify who has made the major contribution to the group's work. Such a growth in scientific research and publication implies unremitting search for financial support for the personnel involved.

65

SUPPORT FOR RESEARCH
IN SCIENCE IN TRINITY

The position of research scientists in Trinity and elsewhere in Ireland in the late 1970s and early 1980s was unenviable. Small pockets of research were funded by research agencies and departments. Support came from the IDA (Industrial Development Authority) and the NBST (National Board for Science and Technology) of which I was a member, but it was small in scale and usually directed to training or other immediately applied objectives. The entire funding and infrastructure of Irish Universities fell far behind European norms. Links between College researchers and overseas groups, in my case with the University of Minnesota, often formed the basis by which researchers could have access to modern facilities which enabled them to stay abreast of their field. The stimulus of working with larger research groups or laboratories and access to some funding were significant. The Irish State offered very little support or encouragement at that time. To be an active research worker one had to find one's own money and equipment. Apart from the US most of my own funding came from the EU for climate-related research. The planes to Brussels frequently carried Irish scientists in search of research support. Even in medical research, professional survival was often achieved through the re-equipping and refurbishing of hospital laboratories from research budgets.

The main forces for progress in the new era were the level of understanding of modern research and its needs which were achieved by residence or visits abroad, particularly to the United States. The Departments of Physics were particularly vigorous and I was able to assist them with additional appointments and, in the case of Genetics, establishing permanent chairs which had not previously existed. One was funded by the generosity of Michael Smurfit, a leading businessman. Appeals to the State to shake off its indifference fell on deaf ears. Instead there was relief that the US and the EU were available to support us.

In 1985 Adrian Phillips, a Fellow in Geology, founded a campus company, ERA/MAPTEC, the success of which led in 1986 to a College policy of formally establishing campus companies and to setting out regulations for the use of intellectual property in a form still in use today. Professors Vincent McBrierty in Physics and Sean Corish in Chemistry played a leadership role in the process. Much credit goes to Eoin O'Neill, Director of Innovation Studies, a post at professorial level, who provided much of the organisational ability, backup and external contacts to drive the development of campus companies and of patenting forward. I was happy to support these developments which led to productive relationships between the College and industry in several fields. I did not fear that this might lead to loss of academic independence, for many scientists are, and will continue to be, 'blue-sky' researchers with a main interest in exploring fundamental questions of intellectual interest that may not have any foreseeable commercial payoff.

In the eighties and into the early nineties physical developments had taken place which laid the foundations for major expansion in research. The O'Reilly Institute, an interdisciplinary research building, was opened in 1987 with generous funding by Tony O'Reilly in memory of his father and mother, John and Aideen O'Reilly, and its adjacent Innovation Centre (IDA-aided) opened in 1989, in time to host the Hitachi Laboratory. The Structural Funds programmes of the EU assisted in the development of the Hamilton Building and the Biotechnology Institute. My own role ceased with the securing of funding for the Hamilton Building, but the College was then well-placed to make major advances as the State finally began to make major research funding available in the last ten years.

BEGINNINGS – A CAREER IN RESEARCH

Teaching and research are intertwined at University. It is impossible to conduct them as independent activities. A young lecturer tends to be heavily burdened with routine tasks while his research takes off slowly. Nobody should underestimate the importance of money in research especially in the sciences and medicine. It is the oil that causes everything to move. In my young days money was so sparse that it required some indulgence from a benevolent supervisor to get off the ground. I was often self-funded from a very meagre base. At least things are much better now, but the struggle is permanent.

I began at Hull, having learned that the University was built on estuarine silt from the River Humber under which, about fifteen feet down, lay a peat-bed. I drilled a hole with a soil-auger to obtain samples and thus my career as a pollen-analyst began. I kept in touch with Frank Mitchell who arranged for me to go to Cambridge to spend a few days in the laboratory run by Sir Harry Godwin, then Professor of Botany and with his assistant Donald Walker, a Fellow of Clare College, who taught me many useful skills. Donald subsequently emigrated to Australia's National University at Canberra where I visited him several times and examined students for him.

My mind was turned to Ireland, however, and the interglacial deposit at Kilbeg, County Waterford, near Kilmacthomas, about which I had heard Frank Mitchell lecture when I was an undergraduate. The deposit was a peat and marl bed about twenty feet below the surface buried by boulder clay. It had been exposed by digging a well-shaft for a nearby dairy co-operative. The drilling was very difficult with many large rocks to negotiate. Our driller's job was to sink well-shafts. He had a vocabulary of amazing range and foulness. Over a period of a few weeks Frank and I managed to obtain samples from drilling and from residual materials of the earlier excavation. The samples available were somewhat unsatisfactory but proved very rich in fossil seeds and fruits which I studied with excitement.

The species included *Daboecia cantabrica*, a heather now found only in Galway and Mayo in northwest Europe and not spotted by Knud Jessen, Professor of Botany at Copenhagen University, amongst his material from an interglacial deposit he was studying from near Gort in County Galway. He had also named a new species, *Menyanthes microsperma*, from his collection. *Menyanthes* is the bog-bean, a common species of Irish wetlands. A few years later after some experience in North America I realised that the 'new species' was actually a common North American aquatic, which no longer occurs in Europe, in the same family as *Menyanthes*. Jessen, always very friendly, was full of congratulations. The Kilbeg work (in my list of cited publications) should have been examined for a Ph.D. but Frank derided (wrongly, in my view) higher degrees and said that publication was all that counted. Americans, however, regard a Ph.D. as the 'union card'. It was not until 1973 that I submitted my published work for a Trinity D.Sc. which was awarded. Subsequently I was awarded honorary doctorates in Laws from Queen's University and in Sciences from the National University.

Frank had been Research Assistant to Professor Jessen. In the early 1930s Jessen was commissioned by the Royal Irish Academy to study the history of Ireland's vegetation cover since the Ice Age by studying the fossil flora contained in peat bog profiles. This included pollen-analysis (originally called pollen statistics), the counting of large numbers of fossil pollen grains, which preserve very well in peat and lake sediments, are varied in form from species to species and are even beautiful morphologically, so that there is an aesthetic pleasure in counting them. Pollen does not survive oxidation — successive wetting and drying — but will last indefinitely in wet conditions and is easily extractable by standard chemical procedures.

Jessen's specialisation, however, was the study of fossil seeds and fruits (macrofossils) at which he was a great expert. Frank followed and sustained this tradition and transmitted it to me. As I began my work, developments in pollen analysis had made the Geological Survey in Copenhagen a world-leader in the subject. There Johannes Iversen brought the critical study of pollen morphology to a high peak in microscopy. Earlier, a limited range of pollen types was counted routinely, others were omitted, and as most pollen in temperate northern latitudes comes from trees this was considered sufficient, but in the Iversen era all types were pursued with the greatest rigour. A famous text-book by Iversen and his Norwegian

69

colleague Knut Faegri became the starting point for research in Quaternary pollen analysis, and Copenhagen became the place to be for the ambitious scientist. Iversen and Frank had maintained contact, their friendship dating to a conference in Ireland which brought Europe's pollen analysts together for the first time since the war. I had the good fortune to spend three weeks in Copenhagen shortly after I had returned to Dublin and had an introduction to the new, more rigorous, pollen-analysis by Iversen's distinguished junior colleague, Svend Th. Andersen. At the same time another Dane, J. Troels Smith, showed how the role of prehistoric people in forest clearance could be inferred from pollen counts which recorded common weeds and cereals as fossils.

The emphasis on critical pollen analysis and its utility in archaeology made the Jessen tradition seem outdated at first but seeds and fruits provide information that cannot be obtained from pollen, especially in identification of species when pollen often cannot be carried below genus or family level. There are also species which produce abundant seeds but very little or poorly preserved pollen. In effect the two types of study are complementary. I have tried to apply both techniques to cores I have studied. It yields a big increment of knowledge. To perform effectively in these fields one needs to build up large reference collections but, above all, to know and remember large numbers of plant species in the field and to have a personal memory bank for their pollen and seed morphology.

Much research depends on exact chronology, most usually obtained by the technique of radiocarbon dating. Trinity was an early performer in the late 1950s in this field. The scientists involved were Cyril Delaney and Ian McAulay of the Physics Department, who constructed and tested the dating apparatus (see Bibliography). A significant number of dates was obtained on both peats and archaeologically significant materials such as charcoal from prehistoric tombs. The project came to an end from endemic lack of resources and a desire of the physicists to move on from simply providing a service for producing dates.

Nowadays radiocarbon dating has largely moved out of the

universities to large commercial laboratories or state institutions, the major ones being located in the United States. Not surprisingly, some of the basic assumptions of radiocarbon dating such as the constant flux of radiocarbon in the atmosphere, proved over-simplistic. Much effort now goes into the counting techniques and great care is taken in the selection of material to be dated. The technique now in use is most usually accelerator mass spectrometer dating (AMS), which permits dating of small samples (seeds, charcoal, and wood fragments) rather than the larger bulk samples of the past. The AMS dates are calibrated to calendar years by complex computer procedures which have been developed in the last decade.

IRELAND

It is impossible in a book like this to write comprehensively about my research. This would require another and probably longer one. Instead, a few examples, one from Ireland, one from Italy and one from the United States, will show how my work developed with the passage of time and the emergence of new opportunities.

I will begin with the famous (in my field) Younger Dryas Period, a time of some 500 years at the transition from the end of the Last Glaciation to the Post-Glacial period. *Dryas octopetala* (mountain avens), is a beautiful white-flowered low-growing shrub, which can be seen in Ireland today in western limestone areas, especially in the Burren region. Throughout the world it and closely related species are mainly found at high elevations in alpine regions or in Arctic lowlands. In Ireland it is a survivor from the last glaciation, growing in rocky places where there is little competition from woodland. Its geological importance first came to light at a brickyard near Copenhagen (Allerød), where its fossil leaves were found in a clay overlying other more organic deposits which suggested a warmer climate. *Dryas* has tough scalloped leaves, rather like those of the oak, which make good fossils. It was supposed, I suspect on lesser evidence, that a basal clay also contained Dryas leaves, hence the

71

upper clay and the time of its sedimentation became known as the Younger Dryas Period.

When Knud Jessen came to Ireland in the 1930s with Frank Mitchell as his field assistant, one of the sites he investigated was at Ballybetagh near Glencullen in south County Dublin, where fossil giant deer (*Megaloceros*) had been found in considerable quantity in a small boggy marsh. He excavated the site and discovered that the deer were found in rather organic deposits buried by clay, which contained seeds and leaves of Arctic plants, especially leaves of the dwarf willow *Salix herbacea*. He drew attention to the comparison with the Younger Dryas deposits in Denmark.

In the following years it became apparent that Younger Dryas deposits were widespread in Ireland and Britain (Ballybetagh was the first to be identified in either island). It could be demonstrated that fossil deer were found under Younger Dryas sediments when the stratigraphy was adequately investigated. It came to be accepted that extinction of the deer was caused by the climatic deterioration of the Younger Dryas period. Our present understanding is that at the end of the Last Glaciation, about 13,000 years ago, the climate warmed quickly and organic lake muds were deposited in lakes and ponds. At this time there was rich grassland everywhere but trees had not yet arrived because of the time taken to migrate from their glacial refuge areas. The grassland was an ideal environment for large grazing animals. Then the climate suddenly became colder once more, the grassland cover was very greatly reduced and silt, clay, and small stones slumped into lake basins because of frost disturbance of the soil. This is the Younger Dryas Period in which the giant deer became extinct because its food resource was so diminished. Hunting played no role because humans had not yet come to Ireland and there is little evidence for major predators. Dryas leaves, by the way, are not particularly common in Ireland, except in limestone regions. The dwarf willow is the real marker of the period. It still occurs on our higher mountains.

Subsequently, there was much discussion of how widely the Younger Dryas episode could be found. I believed it was restricted to western Europe and published a paper to that effect, but I was wrong, it was simply not researched enough then. We now know that Younger Dryas sediments can be identified throughout the North Atlantic region and perhaps more widely. It can be identified with certainty in southern Italy and Florida and as a climatic event in ice cores and ocean cores. It was clearly an event of huge regional importance.

The Younger Dryas presents interesting and unanswered scientific problems. It was plainly a climatic reversal to cold, after a brief, but strong, warming at the end of the Last Glaciation. Its chronology is well established but precisely why did it happen at all? It began and ended suddenly, in decades rather than centuries, a sobering thought at times of concern for climatic change. Its deposits are found at the base of our lakes and ponds but it also caused small glaciers to form. At Lough Nahanagan in the Wicklow Gap south of Dublin the end moraine of a small corrie glacier lies under the lake's surface — it was exposed when the lake level was lowered during construction of a pumped storage scheme for electricity generation. The moraine is of Younger Dryas age. It contains blocks of organic material formed in the Late Glacial lake which were ploughed up by the developing glacier. Was there some explanation other than lack of grazing for the disappearance of the giant deer. After all, it had survived the main glaciation. How? Where? There are still problems to struggle with in the study of this fascinating time.

ITALY

In Italy we had the good fortune to find a very important lake site in the centre of the peninsula, near the town of Melfi, about 100 km east of Naples. The circumstances were that Professor Brian Huntley of the University of Durham, a post-doctoral student of mine in Dublin at the beginning of his career, and his colleague Judy Allen and I, working with a grant to me from the European Climatology Programme, were looking for a site to study in Italy. It was part of a plan, which ultimately proved over-ambitious, to

73

make a transect of perhaps five sites in Europe from south to north for a comparative study of their forest history. Much of our field-work was unproductive until Brian and Judy returned from Italy with a 25.5m core taken from the swampy margin of Lago Grande di Monticchio (Lake Monticchio for brevity). Some lakes, of which Lake Monticchio is one, provide especially favourable environ-ments for detailed chronological study. These are usually deep lakes without inflowing streams and protected from strong winds by natural features which permit sedimentation in calm water without disturbance. In such an environment sediments may be deposited as annual couplets in which the spring and later summer productivity of the lake are distinctive in composition and colour. In some lakes the spring/summer colour distinction is so great that the cores appear zebra-striped but, more commonly, as at Lake Monticchio, the seasons have different shades of brown. They are visible to the naked eye or can be seen in thin section under the microscope. The annual couplets (laminae, bands or varves) can be counted and can yield an exact chronology over long periods of time. Varve-counting can be demanding and time-consuming. It requires skill and dexterity in preserving and mounting the cores for study.

Lake Monticchio resulted from a very large volcanic explosion which took place about 130,000 years ago according to the opinion of Italian volcanologists, whose estimate corresponds with our independent results. It is an ideal study site with no inflowing streams and it is protected by the forested steep walls of its crater. After the original explosion created a lake basin, it filled with water, and sediment was deposited until today, when the lake is not even 10 metres deep. Cores from the lake reveal long periods of varve formation. In addition, the sediments contain numerous volcanic ash horizons which are datable by direct study of the larger ashes and by comparison with already dated volcanic deposits from elsewhere in the region. The distinctive geochemical characteristics of the ashes in the Lake Monticchio core point to the source volcano, in nearly all cases from the Naples/Vesuvius area.

I studied the first 25.5m core collected in 1983 from the

marginal swamp of Lake Monticchio making use of pollen and plant macrofossil analysis. The resulting publication in 1985 was rather unsatisfactory because of dating difficulties, subsequently overcome by newer technologies and a better choice of material to date. The core clearly recorded the last 13,000 years (Postglacial/Holocene and Late-Glacial) and a long earlier record where the age was still obscure. The site was discussed at several conferences where a variety of opinions was expressed. One of the outcomes was an approach from a German group, based on the GeoForschungsZentrum (GFZ) geological research centre at Potsdam near Berlin, under the leadership of Professor Jörg Negendank and with several highly skilled younger colleagues, among whom Bernd Zolitschka was prominent in our early years of cooperation. The involvement of the GFZ was critical because it was very well equipped and experienced in taking long cores throughout the world. It was also well supported financially. The lake was cored from the surface in several expeditions to 70m and finally, in 2000, to 102.3m (about 336 feet). I participated in the work until the late nineties but had retired before the final very deep core was obtained. My contribution was to study the pollen and plant macrofossils of the first 50m and of some of the still older sediments and to study and record the species composition of the surrounding oak and beech forest which was necessary for the interpretation of the pollen counts.

For the larger cores, drilling was carried out from a large platform which had been towed to the lake centre and anchored by ropes to the shore. The lake is shallow, less than 10m deep and nearly 1km long. Cores were taken in 3m increments with a sampling tube of 10cm diameter with reduction in diameter as the bottom was approached. Driving down and lifting the coring rods was carried out with the aid of a small engine. Casing was used at the highest levels to ensure that the coring is carried out vertically in the same hole at each drive. The coring rods were screwed together and taken apart by a drilling team as the sampler was alternately lifted out and then thrust down to the next level. Coring is a heavy job physically and can use every possible mechanical aid. In the last coring effort in 2000, already mentioned, at the depth of 102.3m the rocky bottom of the basin was reached. This was a remarkable achievement for, at such great depths, the chance of equipment failure is high. One must envisage the sausage-like cores placed end to end as being longer than a full size football pitch.

The cores are dark-brown when predominately organic, which indicates a warm temperate climate at the time of deposition, and lighter-coloured with a higher inorganic component of silt and clay during cold periods. They show signs of annual banding for long periods and also layers of tephra (volcanic ash) varying from microscopic to obvious to the naked eye. There are eleven marker tephras, thick layers which can be dated. They play an essential part in establishing the chronology of the site. One, at 56,000 years old, is 30cm thick, and must have been disastrously destructive over large areas. The astonishing number of 340 tephra layers has been identified in the longest core, testimony to the persistence and frequency of volcanic eruptions in southern Italy.

We now know probably more in detail about climate and vegetation cover in the last 130,000 years in southern Italy than anywhere else in the world. Quite simply, nothing comparable is known anywhere else. It is a world-class site of great importance to climate history. It is the only site known where a complete glacial-interglacial cycle has been studied in such great detail.

In broad outline what has been established is that, after a period of extreme cold, the Last Interglacial warm period with climatic characteristics like the warm interglacial in which we live, began about 127,000 years ago and lasted for 17,000 years. The present warm period (Post-glacial or Holocene) began approximately 11,000 years ago, preceded by a brief warm/cold oscillation (ending with the Younger Dryas episode). It followed the last period of severe glacial cold which ended the complete glacial/interglacial cycle. The Last Interglacial was followed by two long near-interglacial warm phases, separated from each other by short cold episodes. The major cold phase which followed began about 83,000 years ago. It was a time of variable environments with some partially wooded periods but never fully forested, as in the warm phases, and always with some steppe or grassland. The very cold 10,000 or so years before the Late-glacial and Holocene was treeless in southern Italy with herb-rich steppe-like grasslands. The climatic information inferred from pollen and plant macrofossil analysis is placed in a very detailed time frame based on annual laminae, radio-carbon dating, tephrochronology (dating by volcanic ashes) and several other technologies[1] such as Argon/Argon ($^{40}Ar^{39}Ar$) dating. The broad characteristics of the climatic events known in detail from Lake Monticchio can readily be closely linked chronologically to comparable sequences recorded in marine cores from the North Atlantic, ice cores from Greenland and lake cores from Florida. What has been discovered is not just valid for southern Italy or western Europe, but for the whole North Atlantic region, east and west. The wider interactions with adjoining continental regions and, especially, comparison with information from ice cores from Antarctica are currently active topics of study.

NORTH AMERICA

In 1961 I received an invitation from Professor Herbert E. Wright Jr (Herb) of the University of Minnesota to spend a period of study in his laboratory, funded by the local Hill Family Foundation, and to deliver a course on biogeography to graduate students. My research was to study plant fossils, especially seeds, from peat and lake sediments in Minnesota. Herb was building up what developed into one of the leading groups of Quaternary scientists in North America, partly by inviting European scientists to work as part of his research group and to share their skills. My travel to Minnesota was funded by our own Scholarship Exchange Board. Gerry and our two little boys, Niall and Michael, came too. Our daughter Sheila was born in 1963 after we returned to

---

[1] Detailed references to new technologies used can be found in papers listed in the Bibiography (Braurer et al. 2007)

Ireland. We arrived at the end of December 1961 and were exposed to the possibilities of the Minnesota winter which became very familiar in subsequent visits. There was snow on the roof of our rented house from January to April, and temperatures could be very low, 10°F to 20°F being common-place. If a wind-chill factor is added, on very cold days it was possible to have air temperatures of -20°F to -30°F and on one memorable day to -70°F. At these temperatures ice more than a metre thick forms on lakes and the ground is deep-frozen.

My first Minnesota field-trip took place to core a lake on St Patrick's Day 1962, when I spent a night in a sleeping bag half buried in a haystack to keep the very cold wind at bay. A farmer drove his tractor over the ice to see what we were doing. Buildings in the Twin Cities of St Paul and Minneapolis had giant icicles hanging from the cornice. Ice crackled and groaned underfoot on the pavements but, to the experienced, a metre of ice was plenty to hold up a truck and we would drive on to lakes to set up our coring apparatus in order to sample sediments reached by chopping a hole in the ice. Minnesota has a short spring when everything comes to life very quickly and a summer when thunderstorms are common, with mosquitoes to keep one indoors. I preferred the decidedly bracing winter climate and, in later visits, often travelled in January, to a brisk working climate which suited my Trinity schedule. I made an arrangement with College by which, when I was Dean of Science, I would be funded to travel to the US for a period of four weeks annually.

My research progressed well with Herb so that a second visit in 1963 was easy to arrange. It established a pattern. I have visited the US once or twice annually ever since and about half of my seventy or so publications are based on US work. Herb was very helpful to me. We went on field trips together or with others on numerous occasions. He loved coring and was constantly improving his apparatus or improvising to overcome difficulties. I learned to core from him during field-work. Most of our later field-work in the ice-free south-eastern US was done on lakes. We would lash two boats or canoes together and construct a coring platform of planks or hardboard on top, then put a sampler and rods down with casing around them to make sure that the coring apparatus always went in to the same vertical hole. This requires a very well anchored system to prevent the platform moving. We could core manually to depths of 40 metres (20 metres of water, 20 metres of sediment), taking a one metre core with each drive. It is hard physical work but perfectly possible.

After first studying sites in the Mid-West my ambition turned to work in Florida, attractive because very largely unstudied and close to the tropics. The tropic of Cancer lies between southern Florida and Cuba and truly tropical vegetation is found in the southernmost fifth of Florida with trees such as royal palm, mahogany and gumbo-limbo (*Bursera*) on drier ground with much wetland vegetation and mangrove swamps in the Everglades. I had learned from colleagues in Minnesota that a line of study sites in a transect across an ecotone (a region where one major vegetation type grades into another, as with the prairie-forest border in Minnesota) would reveal climate change as the invasion of one type of vegetation by another. Would Florida reveal a northward migration of tropical trees up the peninsula in a warming climate or a southern invasion of broad-leaved trees in a cooling climate, as glaciers covered the Mid-West and North-East? These broad biogeographic questions came to be re-phrased with the developing of a new focus of scientific interest on questions of climate change. Herb and I with Eric Grimm, a Minnesota graduate now based at the Illinois State Museum at Springfield, cored Lake Tulane at Avon Park south of Orlando and close to the present northern limit of tropical vegetation. Eric is a first-class corer with special skills in fixing the position of platforms using sacks of sand to serve as anchors.

Lake Tulane is a limestone sinkhole (karst) lake without an inflowing stream. There are many such in the Florida Peninsula. We took the first core in 1992 and a larger team later obtained 8 cores from the north basin of the lake, two duplicated to provide for overlapping cores to ensure completeness of the record. The water depth is about 20m and the sediment thickness is 20m. The master-core dates from the present to 60,000 years ago; not so old as our Italian site and without annual laminae or volcanic ashes but still rich in information and providing more complete detail for 60,000 years than any other site in the US. The glacial-age pollen record from Tulane shows an alternation of domination by pine pollen with phases dominated by oak, *Ambrosia* (ragweed) and grasses. Pine dominance points to high water as today with high lake levels, oak points to a much drier climate with lowered lake levels. The Holocene (Post-Glacial) begins with oak domination but the last six or seven thousand years is dominated by pine with high water-levels and the development of huge swamps.

The biogeographic questions raised are easy to answer from Tulane and other sites. Tropical forest trees never moved up the Florida Peninsula in the last 60,000 years, perhaps permanently limited by occasional winter invasions of cold air from the Canadian Arctic as can still happen today, destructively for citrus cultivation. Central Florida's flora was largely made up of species, which are common today, throughout the whole 60,000 years. There was no presence of broad-leaved deciduous trees in any number before 15,000 years ago. Then, quite quickly, but restricted to northern Florida, a species-rich forest with oak, beech, hickory, hornbeam and a diversity of other trees appeared about 13,000 years ago. This was an important source area for the trees which would now migrate northwards and form the modern high forests of the eastern and mid-western Unites States and Canada. Beech is particularly interesting. It still occurs in large stands along the Florida-Georgia state line, but one or two isolated pockets still occur further south, relics of the period when migration began.

What of the climate record from Tulane? It is of great interest and importance because its chronology has been studied with meticulous attention to detail with 55 radiocarbon dates. Dates older than 40,000 years are unreliable because they have reached the technical limit for radiocarbon dating but some 40 younger dates are reliable. However, the pine and oak peaks in the pollen data clearly can be aligned with similarly-aged climatic events recorded in North Atlantic ocean cores and in ice-cores from

Greenland. On land, similarly aged events can be detected in the southern Italian records from Lake Monticchio. It seems that climatic fluctuations have a broadly similar structure, timing and duration in the North Atlantic and on the continents to its east and west. Absolute identity of the timing of climate events cannot be claimed without further enquiry, and caution is necessary, but there are undoubtedly many common features in all the data sets available. The climatic questions are complex in detail and beyond the scope of this book. Sources of information about Lake Tulane can be found in the Bibliography.

As well as Florida, I also worked in the Pacific Northwest. I was invited to be a visiting professor at the Quaternary Research Center in the University of Washington at Seattle in 1978 and spent a packed month there giving seminars and looking at research possibilities. One of the students who attended my course, Cathy Whitlock, joined me in the field to learn coring. We explored quite large areas of the Pacific Northwest in 1978 and in subsequent visits looking for suitable study sites. Cathy and her then husband, Tony Barnosky, a palaeontologist, spent summers in the Grand Teton and in Yellowstone National Parks where I visited them. Both Cathy and Tony spent a year as postdoctoral fellows in Trinity in 1983. Tony carried out distinguished research arising from excavation of giant deer remains from Ballybetagh near Dublin. Cathy studied a Late-glacial site in the Dingle peninsula and spent some time in Minnesota taking course work in palynology under E. J. Cushing, who had himself studied under Iversen in Copenhagen, and was subsequently an important teacher and mentor to Minnesota students. The Minnesota connection has made a network of continuing friendships in North America. Cathy subsequently became a Professor at the University of Oregon and later at the State University of Montana at Bozeman near Yellowstone. She has had a distinguished career and a strong record of published research, with a special interest in fire ecology and its interaction with forest history at Yellowstone National Park and in South America. Fire history can be inferred from charcoal and pollen in lake sediments.

LAST REFLECTIONS

There are innumerable sites where pollen-analysis can be carried out, but the essential issue for the scientist today is to identify the ones most capable of yielding a rich variety of information. If you want long records you must turn your back on the glaciated areas like Ireland which, by definition, cannot yield long unbroken sequences. The tropics provide a constant temptation but, except at high elevations, are difficult to work with because of the number of species involved, the necessity to build large reference collections and the sheer difficulty of field work in intractable and inaccessible places. Pollen-analysis there may have to give way to other techniques which yield less detailed but critical information more rapidly and more cheaply.

What is the fascination of this type of study which has lasted throughout my life? It is a combination of the intellectual and aesthetic pleasure of identifying pollen and fossil seeds and fruits. It requires a mind that has a large memory-bank for shape, decoration, and size, the sort of memory which, faced with an unknown, asks where did I see that before? Is it completely new to me, and what are the possibilities which I should check? It involves field work, often in remote places, and can be almost anywhere in the world. It needs an experienced eye for landscape so that sites worthy of study can be identified. Above all the investigator must remember that there is no point in producing a huge volume of data for its own sake. What is important is the quality of the question being asked and its potential for an interesting answer.

Leaving aside the strictly scientific issues, the subject offers many experiences and pleasures that are not open to the laboratory-bound scientist. There is the sense of buried treasure as one opens a core to see something quite new, a new volcanic ash, a dramatic change in sediment and perhaps, more romantically, the sheer pleasure of wild and beautiful places; at Monticchio, forest floors covered with *Cyclamen*, and nightingales everywhere; in Florida, wonderful birds and the speculative look on the large alligator which watched us as we cored in a cypress swamp. These compensate for all the duller days and leave wonderful memories.

7.
AN OFFICER OF THE COLLEGE

ADMISSIONS

IN JANUARY 1970 PROVOST McConnell invited me to become Senior Lecturer in place of Frank Mitchell who had resigned from the post. Although the College has many senior lecturers, the ancient title Senior Lecturer belongs to an Annual Officer appointed by the Board following nomination by the Provost. The Board may oppose the Provost's nomination, but this rarely occurs and I was duly appointed. The Senior Lecturer is secretary to the Academic Council and has a wide range of responsibilities for the organisation of teaching within the College, the administration of examinations and admission to undergraduate study. Admissions provided a whole range of intractable problems.

After the war years, when I was an undergraduate (1948–53), College had a very diverse student body. There was a large contingent of British students, a significant number of whom had seen war service, including Polish men and women, who were unable to return to their now Communist-governed native country. Many of the Poles emigrated finally to Canada. There was a large group from the British colonies, soon to become independent nations, especially from Nigeria and south-east Asia, together with many Northern Irish students, mainly from Protestant schools. Protestants from the Republic, the traditional mainstay of the College, and those few Catholic citizens of the Republic who had evaded or ignored the hostility of their church to the College completed the numbers. Many older graduates think of this as a golden time when the College was very cosmopolitan in its student body, but the historical circumstances which made for this mix were soon to change irreversibly.

Within a few short years the ex-servicemen had gone, citizens of new nations were educated at home for the most part, and the expansion of the university system in Britain made for more choice and less incentive to come to Ireland. A major source of students from Northern Ireland disappeared with the opening of the New University of Ulster at Coleraine in 1968 and the transfer there of students from Magee University College who formerly came to Trinity for the third and fourth year of study for the BA degree. This source of northern students had finally dried up by early 1972. The siting of the new university was a serious grievance to nationalists and to those unionists who thought the university should have been based in Derry but it is often overlooked that the decision seriously diminished Trinity's role as a bridge between North and South. Many of the older generation of Presbyterian clergy, for example, took their BA degrees in Trinity, a practice now largely lapsed.

The College, thus faced with the loss of several of its sources of students and a diminution of others, was struggling for its very existence. In the mid-fifties the number of students fell from above 2,000 to below that figure; by contrast it had reached 15,300 in 2006. There were simply not enough Protestants, independent Catholics and others, for the College to survive, much less expand and develop. Some County Councils even refused to allow their university awards to be held in Trinity on the grounds that we did not have a requirement for Irish as a compulsory admission subject. This decision was made by Councils, many of whose members could not speak Irish or use it in the conduct of their business. The consequence was that Protestant winners of County awards were effectively directed to attend colleges of the National University. I was working in a laboratory under the direction of my mentor Frank Mitchell who was Registrar at the time. I remember that he was depressed one afternoon on his return from a Board Meeting, saying that, without more Irish students, the very future of the College was in doubt. He persuaded the College to introduce a policy of limiting student numbers from outside Ireland to free-up places for the anticipated growth in Irish student numbers, which indeed took place subsequently. This was a very unpopular policy with loyal graduates overseas who wished to send their children to their old college.

The College's difficulty was with John Charles McQuaid, the Catholic Archbishop of Dublin, who denounced Trinity annually in Lenten Pastorals as an unsuitable establishment for Catholics to attend, thus reinforcing 'the ban' sustained by the Catholic Hierarchy since the nineteenth century. Many Catholics found 'the ban' embarrassing but most felt bound by their church's policy. However, help came from a number of unexpected sources. In an increasingly independent climate of thought, there was a steady increase in demand for places from Catholic students who were prepared to ignore 'the ban' and who already perceived that their church's position was ceasing to be sustainable. From 1962 onward, the Second Vatican Council had a very large liberalising influence of which Trinity was one of the beneficiaries.

The final breakthrough came in 1967 when Donogh O'Malley, then Minister for Education, announced with little or no consultation that Trinity and University College Dublin (UCD) were to be united in one university. The 'merger' proposal caused uproar among the academic staff of the two colleges but it completely undermined 'the ban' because, for example, one proposal was that law should be united in Trinity. Would legal education in Dublin be available to Protestants only? It was clearly an untenable position. The Catholic bishops, collectively, finally removed 'the ban' on the 25th June 1970. As Senior Lecturer I received a letter on the following day from a Catholic would-be student wanting to be the first post-ban admission. In fact, the number of Catholic students was already growing considerably and the rising tide became a torrent eventually, as the effects of the introduction of free secondary education during 1967 came through. Lest I seem obsessed with religious affiliation, which had an obvious historical importance, I do not believe that religious affiliation should play any part in selecting candidates for university places or posts. When I was Provost I brought the recording of religious affiliation to an end as I viewed it as a matter for private conscience outside the College's remit.

FOUNDING THE CENTRAL APPLICATIONS OFFICE

Although the great growth in student numbers was still to come, the admissions system was already under strain in the early seventies. In particular, application to Trinity's and UCD's medical schools were often from the same people and there was no procedure by which preference could be established. Hasty exchanges between College Green and Belfield of the type 'are you offering to Kelly, J. and has Smith, W. accepted a place?' were only just tolerable as a procedure. If both Colleges made offers to the same very talented students only, no offers might be made to perfectly adequate students when places were still available.

At that time Trinity required a school report, intended to be rather comprehensive, on the academic promise of the potential student. This was a well-known procedure for Northern Irish and English universities which issued place offers based on the report together with an interview, and set a level of performance which guaranteed a place if achieved. We did not have the resources to conduct interviews, which are potentially very expensive and time-consuming, but the system was also failing with the Republic's Catholic schools which were unused to the report system and would write impossibly short references. Conscientious nuns always found the best in their girls while one Irish-speaking boys school had only one reference — *buachaill ar fheabhas* (an excellent boy), perhaps a tongue-in-cheek testing of Trinity's suspected linguistic incompetence.

At the same time computers were rapidly becoming important

and our applicants were recorded on huge computer print-outs. With no real competence in computing — it still escapes me — it was yet easy to see in principle that admissions could readily be processed by computer, making use of Leaving Certificate results. The principle was simple. Applicants for university admission would be permitted to record ten choices of College plus course in order of preference and they would be admitted to the highest choice to which their Leaving Certificate performance entitled them. Thus, an applicant who wished to study medicine could apply to all four of the medical schools then in the system in order of choice and could follow these by other subject choices up to a total of ten. The best achieving students would gain their first choice, others might have to settle for lower choices or, if their objective was simply to go to a particular College, they could accept offers at lower levels of preference.

Long discussions followed early in the seventies between representatives of the Colleges. Liam Barrett, then Assistant Registrar of UCC, Joe McHale, Secretary/Finance Officer of UCD, Séamus Ó Cathail, Academic Secretary of UCG, and Michael Doherty of Trinity, a computer specialist, were usually present. I chaired the meetings. Martin Newell, the future Chief Executive of the Central Applications Office (CAO) was seconded to us from Trinity in December 1975. The discussions were sometimes difficult and tough and seemed to be going nowhere. They had been interrupted in 1974 when Leland Lyons became Provost in Trinity and I resigned as Senior Lecturer to facilitate him in making his own choice of Annual Officers. After an interval the new Provost invited me to continue the discussions and to bring them to a conclusion.

Cork, Galway and Trinity led the debate with UCD hesitant but, in fairness to UCD, the reservations expressed were very pertinent and could not be avoided. It was clear that Trinity's system of asking for school references would not be followed by the other Colleges and could not be built into a new system for one College only without causing extreme distortion. References were favoured in theory by Trinity's Academic Council but most Council members had no hands-on experience of the difficulties they caused. With some reluctance Trinity agreed to abandon references and to adopt a scoring system based on the Leaving Certificate results similar but not identical to those already in use in the NUI Colleges — the famous or infamous Points System, depending on your viewpoint. With the principles agreed, and with excellent support from Tarlach (Terry) Ó Raifeartaigh (Chairman) and Jim Dukes (Secretary) of the Higher Education Authority (HEA) which provided start-up funding, the CAO was launched. Its Articles of Association, of which I wrote the first draft, made it a company limited by guarantee, owned by the Colleges collectively, and independent in its operation.

I became the first Chairman. I like to record that I was supported in becoming Chairman by Joe McHale, saying that he would not trust just anybody from Trinity but that he would give me his trust. I still cherish this as a very great compliment. Representatives were appointed by the NUI Colleges, including Maynooth, represented by its then President and future Bishop of Limerick, Dr Jeremiah Newman and by the HEA, represented by its Secretary, Jim Dukes. The CAO Memorandum and Articles of Association were agreed at a meeting of the Committee of Heads of Irish Universities (CHIU) and Mr Dukes on 9th October 1975 and signed on the 19th December of that year. Thus the CAO came formally into being.

Martin Newell transferred from Trinity's Computer Science Department to become Chief Executive and Secretary to the Company. There was some insistence that the new post should be advertised and it was, although Martin had already contributed greatly to the CAO's evolution. He was incomparably the best qualified candidate of those interviewed. He had an added advantage. He already had academic experience of working in both UCD and Trinity. Martin's appointment was, and continued to be, a very great success. He retired late in 2005. Much of the development of the CAO can be attributed to his very high administrative ability and to the skill with which he gained the trust of the secondary schools. For the first year of the CAO's operation Martin and I worked from a temporary office in Clare Street. We tested the new system on data from the previous year. It operated satisfactorily and, for the following year, we took the risk of moving to the new system. It was launched successfully and we did not run into serious snags then or subsequently.

The new Board settled down well. I was amused, when the question of purchasing a more powerful computer arose, that my more revolutionary younger colleagues wished to go back to the Colleges for advice on what to buy, while I insisted that there was no point in having a technically accomplished Chief Executive if he was not to be allowed to make decisions on equipment. The question was decided by a vote. Desmond Connell, then a Professor in Philosophy in UCD, subsequently Cardinal, voted with me as did other older members to gain the decision. We never looked back. Subsequently we gained another first. Martin had carried out research which showed that the postal service was able to deal with the volume of CAO business anticipated, if its office was based in Galway, which was being lobbied for within our organisation. I thought 'Why not?' So the office was established in Galway where it has been ever since. This was one of the earliest decisions to decentralise from Dublin, a procedure with which most Departments of State are still struggling. I resigned as Chairman when our office was established in Galway, my task in getting the organisation going now complete. I was succeeded by Séamus Ó Cathail, Academic Secretary of UCG.

The advantages of the new system were very clear. Anyone could apply to any College and there was no distinction in terms of religious affiliation, gender, race or physical disability. Children from deprived backgrounds or unpretentious schools had exactly the same examination-based chance as anyone else. Over the years it has become clear that the system, in spite of its rather mechanistic aspect, was absolutely fair and that there was no way by which an advantage could be gained by knowing some important public figure. Absolute confidence of fair treatment was and still is a major aspect of its success. The rules were straightforward and could not be bent. The Colleges had the relief that no one could usefully lobby them. When I was in charge of admissions for Trinity I had to deal individually with applications from the children of both the President and the Taoiseach of the day. It is comforting to be able to record that neither attempted to influence the decision in any way whatsoever. It was a relief nevertheless that TDs' 'Green Harp' letters became a thing of the past.

The CAO system has been much criticised. It is not always seen as what it sets out to be, a fair method for sharing out a scarce resource, university places, especially in sought-after faculties such as medicine and law. One simple solution in response to demand is to provide more places by erecting new buildings and creating more teaching posts but, financial constraints apart, this runs into the difficulty that the State or the professions may decide on the desirable number of graduates to produce in particular disciplines, so some must be disappointed even if they have high Leaving Certificate scores. The worst situation is when a number of equal-scoring candidates compete for the last, too few, places and names are chosen by random number, a bitter experience for the losers.

Although several Ministers for Education in recent years have decided that the CAO system should be reviewed and have set up committees to do so, none has come up with a better idea that is relatively inexpensive and equally transparent in operation (a CAO application today costs €35 euro in comparison with a Leaving Certificate cost per candidate of €90 euro). When pressed, many teachers concede that the system is generally accepted as fair. Much criticism of the CAO is based on the pressure to which it exposes students and the competitiveness it generates. Some of the problems arise from the ambitions of parents as much as from the hopes of students. There is a belief that to study medicine or law or other high-demand subjects must naturally be the first choice of school-leavers and some are pressed into subjects for which they have little or no taste, while actually preferring subjects in which places are more easily gained.

There is a tendency to try to beat the system by developing strategies to maximise point scores by identifying supposedly 'easy' subjects. There is now a group of new colleges which specialise in preparing second-chance applicants to the CAO by intensive teaching. It is a financially rewarding business. Some journalists have made a career of advising would-be-students on preparing themselves for university entry and on CAO procedures. Journalists have, in my opinion, contributed significantly to the levels of hysteria, which affect some parents and school-leavers, who find it difficult to make a calm appraisal of their situation. My advice to parents is, within the limits of good sense, to give their children freedom to choose the careers they wish, even if some choices do not promise substantial financial rewards. My advice to Ministers of Education about the CAO and the Points System is to heed the old American saying, 'if it ain't broke, don't fix it', or at least proceed towards change with great caution. It is the best system we have and it has worked successfully for over thirty years.

I believe in equality of opportunity. Much inequality in our secondary schools arises from excessive class size, limits on funding, quality of buildings and equipment and shortage of teachers in some subjects. Schools with limited financial resources may suffer from all of these handicaps in a competitive environment. The best way to promote equality of opportunity is to address these questions which have obvious funding implications. Unless we try to achieve a totally egalitarian society, an impractical objective in my view, there will always be some difference in the quality of secondary school experience between privately-funded schools and schools entirely dependent on the State. The important objective is to come sufficiently close to equality to guarantee everyone a reasonable chance of competing successfully. In the course of its more than thirty years history the CAO has contributed importantly to equality of opportunity. Long may it flourish!

Since I wrote these paragraphs in 2004 a new initiative on numbers to be admitted to medical training has been proposed in a report prepared under the chairmanship of Professor Patrick Fottrell on behalf of the Higher Education Authority. The number of students in medical training annually has been capped at 306 since 1978. Now it is proposed that a total of 725 Irish and EU students should be admitted annually by 2011, four years from now. It is planned that undergraduate admissions will continue to be by existing procedures but that a significant number of graduates in other subjects will be admitted to training in medicine. The problem has been the realisation of the serious insufficiency in graduate output to meet the needs of the medical services. There are many aspects to the proposal which will need further elaboration but the CAO procedures should be sufficient to deal with the mechanical aspects of admission.

At present (2007) it is proposed to admit graduate students to the College of Surgeons and the University of Limerick (which does not have a medical school as yet) in the current year. The NUI Colleges expect to admit both undergraduate students as at present and an additional cohort of graduate students in 2008. Trinity's position is to maintain its present undergraduate procedures and, at least in the short term, not to follow the graduate admissions route. The decisions to be made are still under study by the Higher Education Authority and the Department of Education. It is, in my view, important to retain the transparency of the present CAO procedures with very clear rules governing graduate admissions to avoid any suggestion of unfairness and special treatment for favoured individuals. I shall be glad to be an observer from the touchline of what promises to be a very interesting time.

Ten years as Provost

8.
THE BODY CORPORATE

THE COLLEGE'S STRUCTURE

THE COLLEGE IS GOVERNED by a Board which has responsibility for all major decisions in financial and academic matters alike, though detailed policy and procedures in the academic field are developed by the University Council and reported to the Board. The Board normally accepts the Council's recommendations automatically unless major financial and development issues are involved. The Provost is Chairman of the Board, the University Council and a host of other committees. Annual Officers nominated by the Provost from among senior members of the full-time academic staff sit on the Board. They typically serve for periods of three, four or five years but their appointments must be re-confirmed annually by the Board. The appointments may be challenged by Board members but, although it has been known to happen, they are not normally contested.

Provost McConnell re-nominated his Officers for longer periods, seven years or more, but this became unpopular because it was thought that Officers could become stale on the job and the ambitions of would-be Officers had to be considered. Provost McConnell retired in 1974 at the age of 70 after 22 years in office. A new statute providing for ten-year provostships with retirement by 65 had been introduced. One consequence was that it was necessary to provide shorter terms for Officers for, as the most likely source of future Provosts, they had to be able to demonstrate their ability in office and to acquire a detailed knowledge of the complex business of the College. Then the College would be able to make an assessment of potential candidates when the next election to the Provostship came around. It might be thought that, with a large academic staff, there would be numerous obvious choices for officer posts. In fact, finding Officers is one of the Provost's most difficult tasks. Many able colleagues simply don't want to be Officers because of the potential damage to their academic work and research by the heavy demands on their time. Provosts may find themselves interviewing several colleagues for a post before finding one with some demonstrated administrative ability and a willingness to accept nomination.

The Annual Officers include the Vice-Provost who acts with full powers in the Provost's absence for whatever cause. The nomination of the Vice-Provost is in the sole power of the Provost and, under the College Statutes, cannot be challenged by the Board. Aidan Clarke, who became Lecky Professor of Modern History, was my Vice-Provost for most of my period in office. He was replaced by Professor John Luce, a classicist and a well-known figure as the College's Public Orator, for a two-year period when Aidan first became Head of his department. The Vice-Provost has to be a valued and trusted adviser to be consulted by the Provost when difficulties or problems arise. Aidan played this role very well. His opinion, which he did not often offer, except in response to a direct question, often completed a discussion.

Of the other statutory Officers, the Bursar originally managed the College's finances and investments. Even the most talented amateur could not manage the complexities of the College's finances as the College expanded. A professional accountant, the Treasurer (Franz Winkelmann), was appointed in the 1960s and he continued during my period in office. In keeping with the inexorable growth of the College, the Treasurer's Office has grown from a handful to some 30 staff members today with parallel growth in numbers in other administrative areas. The Bursar's role became to explain the College's financial business to the academic staff and, above all, to play a major part in the development and management of new building programmes.

As already explained elsewhere, the Senior Lecturer is the chief academic officer of the College and secretary to the University Council. Historically, the Registrar kept the Board's minutes and played a major part in degree-conferring ceremonies, but nowadays has acquired a great variety of new duties, especially in relation to associated colleges for which Trinity provides some teaching, and awards degrees. The Senior Dean is responsible for staff discipline and the Junior Dean for undergraduate discipline and rooms allocation. All of these Officers' duties are somewhat fluid and Officers may be given responsibility for new duties or re-assign some of their duties to other members of the administrative staff, an inevitability as the College's activities expand.

In Provost McConnell's time the Provost conducted the College's business through the Officers and the Board. In the 1950s the number of students fell briefly below 2000, was 6,000 when I became Provost and has now grown to over 15,000. Many changes in the structure and administration of the College have been necessary to accommodate this vast growth so that the historic structures and offices have evolved in many ways to embrace new functions or quite new activities. Originally there had been only one faculty Dean, the Dean of Physic (Medicine), Jerry Jessop, who operated so effectively that, on the initiative of Ian Howie, then Registrar, and of myself, the Dean system was extended to the whole College and five new Faculties headed by Deans were created. I served several terms as Dean of Science. The Deans meet regularly under the chairmanship of the Senior Lecturer and are, *ex officio*, members of the University Council. Provost McConnell supported the Faculty initiative, but there was some resistance to what was suspected by some of being an unnecessary innovation. With time the system has become fully accepted and seen as necessary in our enlarged society, although, already in 2005, the re-structuring and redefinition of the College's administrative procedures was under way.

In my time the Annual Officers, the Faculty Deans and the senior professional administrators (Treasurer, Secretary, Librarian and Director of Buildings) met on Friday mornings, weekly or less frequently as need dictated. It gave the College what was essentially a cabinet system of 16 members. It was a good way to ensure that all the members knew what was happening in the College and could exchange views or raise matters of concern. It gave everybody else in the College, in theory at least, but substantially in practice, a route to the centre to express views or receive information. I was aware that communication had been a problem in the College during the era of sit-ins and wanted to be sure that everyone had a reliable source of information in the future. The Friday meetings worked to an agenda and kept minutes. Inevitably they became known to some in the College as the 'Friday fixers'.

Two important offices remain to be mentioned. The Chancellor presides over Commencements (degree-conferring ceremonies) and is the senior Visitor, who shares with another colleague, normally a senior lawyer known as The Visitor, the conduct of hearings into disputes. He or she delivers rulings which are binding on the Board. The Chancellors of my day were the Hon. Frederick Boland, then, on his retirement, Professor W. B. Stanford, who died in office, and finally Frank O'Reilly, a former Chairman of the Ulster Bank. All three were graduates of the College who carried out their duties admirably. On Frank O'Reilly's reaching the statutory retirement age of 75 in 1997 he was succeeded by Mary Robinson who had completed her term of office as President of Ireland.

The Visitor, the Hon Mr Justice Henry Barron, also gave us much of his time. I appeared before him twice while he heard disputes which involved me. I am glad to say that he found for me on each occasion. Once I had vetoed a candidate for a Deanship on the grounds that he did not have sufficient seniority to decide on promotions within his faculty to a standard which he had not himself achieved. The Visitor found that the phrase in the Statutes, 'the Provost having given his consent', did indeed carry the plain implication that consent could be withheld. The other case involved aggrieved mathematicians who objected to being re-located to the back of the College from New Square to enable the Law School to be moved from the overcrowded Arts Building. As I saw it the mathematicians would find themselves close to computer scientists and physicists with whom they had significant common teaching and research interests. My views did not commend themselves to them. The details are tedious and not worthy of repetition here but the Provost did have a statutory right to assign rooms.

I was a keen reader of the Statutes which often provided useful artillery in a dispute. One evolving feature of the Visitor's role is a movement from the informal quick decision-making of the past to a more court-like atmosphere where careful and detailed presentation of documentation and information is required. It is a reflection of the more litigious character of Irish society today that the Visitor's work becomes ever more demanding. Cases may now take up a great deal of time and even lead to representation of parties by Senior Counsel.

In addition to the Chancellor, up to five pro-Chancellors are appointed to deal with the enormous number of Commencements ceremonies that the College requires. Pro-Chancellors are distinguished people in the professions or business or who have led notable lives, excluding only active politicians. They are often, but not necessarily, graduates of the College. As with the Chancellor there is a retirement age of 75. I tried to ensure that at least one Pro-Chancellor was a woman on the grounds that, as up to half of our graduates were women, it was reasonable that they should have the possibility of receiving their degree certificates from one. At present there are two woman Pro-Chancellors and, of course, the Chancellor is Mary Robinson.

In all of these posts the duty falls, in practice, to the Provost and Board to find suitable candidates and seek the approval of the Senate of the University for their appointment. The complex history of the Senate can be found in McDowell and Webb but its main duties relate to the conferring of degrees, including honorary degrees and the approval of new degree courses. Senate meetings tend to be poorly attended, but, on one occasion, Frank O'Reilly's nomination to the Chancellorship was challenged by George Dawson. More than 100 attended the meeting which elected Frank O'Reilly by a substantial margin. The Visitor position was difficult because the appointment was made by the Government by ancient statute which required the submission of two names. One had to find two consenting candidates, one of whom was bound to be rejected. Under new legislation the power of appointing the Visitor reverts to the Board so my successors will not face this difficulty.

THE FELLOWS

Trinity is a Body Corporate made up of the Provost, Fellows and Scholars. The seven most senior Fellows by date of election sat on the Board as of right and the remaining Junior Fellows elected four of their number as members. The number of Junior Fellows was about 30 when I was elected to Fellowship in 1960 and I remember with gratitude that Professor Furlong, then Head of Philosophy ('Mental and Moral Science') took some trouble to introduce me to other Fellows in the Common Room. There are now about 200 Fellows. In my day Fellowship brought a significant improvement in salary but nowadays it has become a question of status and recognition of scholarly achievement only. Under recent legislation the Senior Fellows have lost rights to Board membership and the title retains little real significance. Barbara Wright was the first (and now only) woman to achieve Senior Fellowship in its traditional form before the powers of the position passed into history.

New Junior Fellows are elected annually by the Board on Trinity Monday. Candidates for election are proposed by colleagues and their work is subject to external examination. The criteria for election are publication of research work and being known as an active scholar in one's field. This has the beneficial effect of encouraging and rewarding achievement in research. Negatively the chance that an academic will be elected who is a distinguished teacher but with no research profile is small. I was aware of the problem, widespread in the university system, but did not find a solution. Of course the best scholars are often very good teachers, but excellence in teaching was not rewarded. Since my time a new procedure makes awards annually for high performance in teaching. Academic staff and students alike participate in nominating for awards.

THE ROUTINE OF ADMINISTRATION

I returned from the United States early in September 1981. Leland Lyons retired formally on September 20th and I quickly discovered that nobody expected me to do anything until then. I set myself up in a temporary office and began to read myself into current papers. As Provost I was Chairman of the Board, the Council, the Site Development Committee, the Senior and Junior Promotions Committees and many others too numerous or ephemeral to mention. Decidedly the Provost is both by Statute and custom the College's Chief Executive. The buck stops with him and responsibilities are potentially heavy if things go wrong.

I enjoyed being a chairman and guiding debate to clear decisions. I had had an early minor run-in with Provost McConnell who was apt to let the Board continue from the traditional Wednesday morning into the afternoon and, in extremes, overflowing yet again to Saturday mornings. I thought that Saturday mornings were unnecessary and that discussions should end earlier — he did not agree. Now that my turn had come I stated a policy that the Board would complete all its business on Wednesday mornings and would never, unless in quite exceptional circumstances, meet later in the day or at any other time. I don't think we ever did. I used the mid-morning coffee break to bring minor issues to a decision, threatening cold coffee if we couldn't make up our minds. In my predecessor's day the Board had argued interminably about catering costs which had become a focus for sit-ins and disruption. I ruled that the cost of tomato ketchup sachets and similar items in the

Dining Hall might never again be discussed. More seriously, the Officers agreed to set up a Catering Committee with student representation which defused much conflict because the student representatives could see the reasoning behind pricing and could hope to succeed with some of their own ideas. They had become part of the decision-making and responsibility-accepting process.

My policy was to try to arrive at decisions by consensus. This usually worked because neither the Board nor I were very addicted to conflict. If I saw a serious difference arising my policy was to defer the business and re-introduce it later with whatever modifications were necessary or advisable. Really intractable problems were referred to committees established for the purpose. For example, agreement could not be found on whether to develop land at Trinity Hall for student residences or to retain it as an asset, though what it would then be used for was not at all clear. I asked Brian McMurry, my Registrar at the time, to head a committee to seek views and report them. The outcome was still rather inconclusive, but a major development for residences took place under my successor.

In general I did not favour votes and, after a while, the College Secretary, Gerry Giltrap, stopped bringing the voting book to the Board. One slightly irate colleague demanded on one issue, 'Why can't we decide this by vote?' I said, 'I'll explain afterwards'. I thought voting was potentially divisive, a habit not to be fallen into, creating a taste for party spirit not to be encouraged. Unless I abstained, except for casting votes, I risked the emergence of an opposition, not a possibility to be entertained cheerfully. This may seem too political, even Machiavellian, but it allowed the Board to conduct its business in peace. Anything for a quiet life? Well, nearly. I admired the Spanish prime minister who, asked if it troubled him to be seen as boring and unexciting, replied that it would be a good change from a too exciting recent past. In the outcome, I don't think we had a roll-call vote once in my ten years.

The University Council and Board meetings alternated on Wednesday mornings. There is a significant overlap between the two bodies for the Board must approve financial commitments.

Appointment to chairs (professorships) was specially tedious. Candidates, once a short-list of three to five had been decided on, were interviewed in the morning by a specially appointed selection committee which included external assessors, and then again by the full Council in the afternoon. I chaired both sessions. The Council was unwilling to delegate its function to selection committees and some time was certainly wasted in duplication. Generally, the views of the external assessors were deferred to, though sometimes they were given too much freedom and sometimes were closer to the candidates, for example, as former research supervisors, than was desirable. The effort put into the selection procedure, especially by Gerry Giltrap in briefing and welcoming the candidates, was rewarded by some very good appointments.

Appointments and promotions brought up the question of fair treatment for women candidates and the position of women in College more generally. A committee chaired by Professor Frances Ruane advised the Council and Board. The outcome was that the Council now must be informed of the male/female breakdown in applications for any academic post and also in the shortlist. Each selection committee must have a woman member. This seems to work reasonably well but it imposes a well-known burden on senior woman academics who finish up serving on all too many committees. Shortly after the new procedures were adopted I had to apologise to Council that an all-male committee had met, no appropriate female member being available, but, noting that as they had managed to recommend a woman candidate for appointment, they might be forgiven. Looking around the Common Room today one sees a substantial representation of women staff. With time the proportion of women in senior appointments will increase as promotions of the younger generation take place.

On the subject of the role of women, my wife Gerry played a very important part throughout and was an always steady support during the Provostship. As far as I can see, Provosts' wives scarcely feature in histories of the College; I have found no portraits. There must be photographs, if only of social occasions such as the College Races. A search through newspaper files should reveal something, but it is sparse. Much is expected of Provosts' wives in the social life of the College and in the management of the House. Perhaps that role should receive a greater recognition in future. When we retired we gave a silver dish to the College, following an old tradition. Such dishes adorn the tables for formal College dinners. Ours records both of us in a Latin inscription written for us by John Luce.

FINANCIAL
ADMINISTRATION

The College's finances are managed by the Treasurer and his or her staff. They report to the Board via the Finance Committee. As the Provost does not have a hands-on role in the routine of the Finance Office I confine myself here to a few occasions when my role became more central.

The eighties were a difficult time financially for Trinity. There were problems at national level which led to inadequacies in funding. There was serious inflation such that fees were raised by 30% in one year. Today there are no fees. This has some good aspects but, from the University's point of view, the flexibility to manage income levels from fees was lost and control removed to the Department of Education which may not provide adequate funding. We came to a critical point where it was necessary to try to reduce staffing levels to avoid a financial crisis. Fortunately, the pension fund was very healthy.

The stratagem used was to ask staff members who had reached the age of 60 to consider retirement. They would go on pension, which our rules then allowed, and be re-employed on a part-time basis for a further 2 or 3 years both to protect their income level and their contribution to teaching. In the nature of things some staff members welcomed the opportunity, being ready for retirement, other wished to stay to 65, 67 or 70 as their contract stipulated. Nobody was forced to go.

Posts vacated by retirement remained unfilled for 2 or 3 years but most were eventually re-filled as funding improved. The Board requested that a committee be set up to review priorities in making appointments as conditions permitted and this was done. It was a slow grinding process but was accepted as fair and left few scars. There was some anxiety about the future, particularly among the Library staff who thought they might be specially targeted but I assured them that this was not so and that everybody was being treated on the same basis. There is a strong memory in College that the mid and late eighties were a particularly difficult time financially, but we survived and recovered.

I played a major role in fund-raising, much of it on a personal basis but assisted by George Clarke who ran a small office for the purpose. There was some support from professional fund-raisers but I did not find them very effective. My successor Tom Mitchell set up the Trinity Foundation, which is ably managed by Mary Apied, a more effective and professional way to manage fund-raising in the more prosperous nineties.

I visited the US frequently. One of my trips brought me to see Sir Anthony O'Reilly, Tony O'Reilly as he then was, in Pittsburgh. This led to the successful funding of the O'Reilly Institute. He gave me some good advice, essentially that I had had a success with him but that I had to accept that many of my approaches would be courteously (usually) or rudely (sometimes) refused and that I should not be in fund-raising if I couldn't accept that. I learned not to pursue people for small amounts and, at meetings of graduates, would say that I was not pursuing them for money unless they had a positive wish to give it, but that I wanted them to speak well of their College experience and to value it. I decided to put all my effort into larger amounts, from £10,000 to £1 million, and learned that a donation of £5000 from a London business was a polite indication that no more would come.

There was an illusion in the Department of Education that universities were rich and that the merest shaking of a begging-bowl in the United States should yield substantial wealth. This totally unrealistic view of the difficulty of fund-raising makes one wonder why a State at present unimaginably wealthy, does not do far more to support its universities and why it still thinks the begging-bowl a normal way to raise capital. Success in fund-raising arises from identification of an individual, who has some common interest with you and has altruistic motives. I think I was responsible for raising about £10 million from some six or seven major donors, most of them based in Ireland or with Irish interests. We owe them all our most sincere thanks.

STUDENTS

My own and Gerry's experience teaches me that, to most students, the Provost is a remote figure, not much known, and with a good deal of ignorance about what he actually does. Of course the Provost would know and be known to the current President and Vice-President of the Students' Union who would be in attendance at the Board. There were also student Faculty representatives on the University Council. All had freedom to take part in debates, and exercised that freedom. They did not then have voting rights which are now conferred under new legislation. It was my policy to progress business at Board and Council meetings but, in principle and practice, defended the students' right to speak and ruled that students should not be asked to withdraw from the Board even from sensitive and private business which really was not to be discussed outside. The students honoured this informal protocol which was unenforceable if someone was determined to break it.

Some initiatives I took were primarily of interest to students. There were far too few residential rooms in College. We built new rooms on the Pearse Street frontage some of which overlooked College Park. At the same time we moved the Student Medical Service from cramped quarters in Botany Bay to better accommodation within the new residential block. The service is extremely busy and popular under the direction of Dr David Thomas (retired in 2006) who moved from private practice to take up the position. There had also been a crèche in the Pearse Street houses. It was modified and upgraded to give it more space and increase the number of places, which is still insufficient given that it looks after the needs of both students and staff. I was told that no businessman would give me any money in my fund-raising capacity for a crèche. This may well be true but is short-sighted. I think provision of crèche places is an obvious and increasingly pressing need which universities must address. The crèche was managed by Mrs Imelda Kestell through a committee on which Gerry served.

One initiative arose in 1983 from the film *Educating Rita*, much of which was filmed in College. Michael Caine and Julie Walters starred. There was a scene in the Examination Hall and another in College rooms. For a winter scene buckets of frothy detergent provided plenty of fake snow which reached to the knees on the steps of the Dining Hall. A plaintive Professor Moody wanted to know if this was really necessary as he waded through. The commercial aspect of the film was that for £5,000 a day we would facilitate the filming in any reasonable request. This worked out well for both sides. The film was completed in good time without expensive time-wasting and it continues to be a major success. The College profited to the extent of £100,000. I was just in time to stop the Treasurer from adding the money to the College's general funds. I believed that such an exceptional windfall should be invested for an exceptional purpose. Hence came the Provost's Fund for the Visual and Performing Arts which still continues. It now yields about €21,000 annually.

The income from the Fund has supported many undergraduate activities in music, theatre, film-making and the visual arts. Any student group with a half-reasonable proposal could hope for a hearing. The money was used rather wastefully at times, particularly in film-making but it could be regarded as a learning experience which could provide a basis for future more effective performance. Personally, I specially enjoyed the opportunity to support performances of classical music in the Saloon of the House by small visiting groups or soloists. Professor Hormoz Farhat of the School of Music advised on the programmes and arranged for visits to be made. One such was a performance by Malcolm Proud, a harpsichordist, winner of an Edinburgh Festival competition and a recent music graduate of College. We made a point that students of music were always welcome to attend at no cost to themselves. Many will have seen the Provost's House on such occasions and, I hope, treasured the experience both musically and visually.

I made one important contribution to undergraduate teaching. We had been struggling to teach small groups of freshman students in each of Botany, Zoology, Biochemistry, Microbiology and Physiology. Three of us, Peter Smith-Keary (Botany and Genetics), Billy Roberts (Microbiology) and myself, designed a unified basic Freshman course which would serve as an introduction to all the biological subjects and lead up to subject choice in the two Sophister years. Simultaneously with the development of the new Freshman courses a new well-equipped laboratory was constructed for its practical classes. The laboratory was designed by Billy and Peter, both of whom had very good design skills and a well developed taste for this kind of planning. Billy became Director of the Laboratory. Alas, he died young of a heart attack. The laboratory, now located in the Hamilton building, was named to honour the large contribution he had made to the development of undergraduate teaching.

My research interests did not distance me from teaching. Presenting my own subject and trying to excite others with it as I had been excited in my time gave much satisfaction. I particularly enjoyed field work with undergraduates and graduates alike. I had some very good graduate students who distinguished themselves in their later careers.

In Trinity Week the garden of the Provost's House and the House itself were the focus of a Garden Party organised by a student committee. By tradition ambassadors were invited and most attended, including countries such as the USSR, China and Iran who must have found it a puzzling event but whose representatives were always good-humoured and benevolent. The Party was well-attended and rarely, being in May, was spoiled by impossible weather. For the ambassadors, the formality of the occasion was brought about by the regular attendance of President Patrick Hillery. Paddy Hillery was President during our period in the House. We greatly enjoyed his friendly company and have splendid memories of his dancing on the lawn while the Guinness Jazz Band tootled in the background. We tried to find women students from his home county, Clare, to introduce him to other students present. I'm afraid his successors have taken a more austere view of the event but without the President the party loses some of its effectiveness. It now seems to be passing into history and has not been held in recent years.

I supported sport when possible, urged on by my colleague Trevor West. I had played a few rugby games on Trinity's first team in 1950. I was a front-row forward propping Robin Roe, a behemoth of a man and later an international. He became a Church of Ireland clergyman in due course, though his language in a tough scrum could be somewhat unclerical. I became a Knight of the Campanile, a sporting companionship whose rules I never discovered but who have a very handsome tie. I also supported sport as Provost by being able to produce £10,000 for re-surfacing the tennis courts in Botany Bay, and by dutiful attendance at rowing regattas. I still follow rugby but mostly on television or in the newspapers. I was very pleased when Trinity managed to get into the First Division. With so many professional players and a public demand for quality performance it is difficult for amateurs to stay in touch, and for students, who still have some growing to do, to compete with physically mature opponents.

THE OTHER UNIVERSITIES AND THE HIGHER EDUCATION AUTHORITY

Apart from the heavy social duties of the job the Provost has many duties external to the College in relationship to the State and to sister universities. Our budgets and financial performance required an annual meeting with the Higher Education Authority. This was largely routine but it made opportunities to make cases for new academic developments and building programmes which could be discussed in more detail at subsequent meetings. Close and easy-going contact was maintained. Jim Dukes, the HEA Secretary during much of my Provostship, was a fair-minded and creative public servant. I still remember his phone-calls at the end of the financial year when a little money remained unspent in his budget. 'There's a rattle in the can, Bill', he would declare and we were given permission to pay for some new facility, particularly equipment in the sciences, provided invoices were submitted by a rapidly approaching due date.

The Committee of Heads of Irish Universities (CHIU) met several times a year to discuss policies affecting the universities and to develop common approaches. The original five members were added to when Limerick and NIHE Dublin became full universities. I frequently visited UCD and received hospitality from Presidents Tom Murphy and Paddy Masterson. The Michael Tierney days of root and branch hostility were gone. Part of the original hostility arose from ancient jealousies and from suspicion about access to resources and recruitment of students. Now with better resources and with powerful growth in student numbers everywhere, the edge of competitiveness was blunted and we could discuss common problems in friendship.

Collectively we came under pressure from the Department of Education to increase intake, but our staff-student ratios were very poor so I refused unless there was some matching staff increase. My CHIU colleagues were nervous about this approach, but it was accepted and we were rewarded with significant numbers of 'new blood' appointments, following an earlier British model. Some developing departments gained much-needed staff. I received a medusa look from Mary O'Rourke, then Minister for Education, when I pointed out that Queen's Belfast had two pounds per student to spend for every one we had and wondered which financial practice would prevail when the possible, but not immediately anticipated, day of national unity dawned. I greatly admired Michael Mortell of UCC, then Chairman of CHIU, an annually rotating post, when we called on the Taoiseach, Charles Haughey, to discuss our parlous financial situation. The Taoiseach skated around the issue of money skilfully and suggested that we might save money by leaving chairs such as 'ancient classics' unfilled. As we left President Mortell thanked the Taoiseach and said 'But what we came about was money, more money is what we need'. I don't think it did us much good, but it avoided any pretence that we were satisfied.

MARSH'S LIBRARY

One of the pleasures of being Trinity's Provost is that you become ex-officio one of the Governors and Guardians of Marsh's Library. The Library was founded by Archbishop Narcissus Marsh in 1701, following a period as Provost of Trinity (1679–1683). He viewed his 'rude and ignorant' students with little pleasure and was glad to escape to his books. The Library is in the grounds of St Patrick's Cathedral and historically has been mainly overseen by members of the Chapter of the Cathedral. Originally several high officers of the Crown were Governors and Guardians but most of these offices have fallen into disuse. However, the Chief Justice was also an *ex-officio* member and successful efforts were made to persuade today's Chief Justices to attend.

The Library is presided over by Muriel McCarthy, a very able and popular figure, dedicated to the Library's well-being and bringing it to public attention by excellent exhibitions of the Library's treasures. Much of the collection dates from Marsh's time or shortly thereafter. Élie Bouhéreau, a Huguenot refugee, was the first Librarian. The Library has important Huguenot publications. Bishop Bedell's translation of the Old Testament into Irish is a notable manuscript treasure which Marsh succeeded in publishing in London (1685).

Much of how the Library has increased in stature in the public eye and much lobbying and fund-raising is entirely due to Muriel. In my early years as Provost I helped in some ways, encouraging the American-Irish Foundation to support the Library's activities, increasing to more realistic levels the nearly peppercorn rents of some of the tenants of the Library, so that Muriel's church-mouse salary could be increased to something, if still too small, more appropriate to the work she was contributing. I was keen to see the Library re-painted and the portrait of Marsh cleaned and restored, much of which has happened. Under Muriel's guidance the Library has emerged from an honourable but dusty past into its beautiful present and ever-increasing level of activity. It is now very much better supported by government and the Office of Public Works has helped with structural repairs and re-wiring.

9.
POMP AND CEREMONY

COMMENCEMENTS

ONE OF THE MOST FAMILIAR activities of universities is degree-conferring. In Trinity the Commencements Ceremony is held in the Examination Hall (formally the Public Theatre), a fine 18th century room rich in decorative plasterwork and with large paintings of famous people associated with the College, including the foundress, the first Queen Elizabeth. Students to be 'commenced' appear formally dressed, dinner jackets for men, various black and white themes for women. Gowns and coloured hoods appropriate to the degree and Faculty are worn. Doctoral gowns are scarlet with coloured sleeves. The procession enters, headed by the mace-bearer, then the book porter (carrying not a Bible as many suppose, but the signatures of all the Proctors, the Officers for the ceremony, back to the seventeenth century). Next comes the Caput, the committee of three who preside over the ceremony, consisting, in order of procession, of the Senior Master non-Regent (the most senior Fellow who does not hold an administrative office, a largely ceremonial role), the Provost, and the Chancellor in a specially magnificent gold and black gown. The Chancellor, or Pro-Chancellor, at the centre of the Caput, conducts the ceremony; the Provost, sitting at his or her right, passes the scrolls to be presented by the Chancellor. While the procession arrives the College Organ Scholar plays Bach or other suitable baroque music on the organ in

113

the gallery of the Hall.

The ceremony is still conducted entirely in Latin to the apparent enjoyment and pleasure of the students and, especially, their parents, relatives and friends. Everyone is provided with an account of the ceremony in English, without which it would be incomprehensible to most. In the past Commencements was a time for much horseplay, throwing of bags of flour, even of graduates themselves into a horse trough which existed by the Campanile in my undergraduate days. Nowadays, bobbing and bowing to the Chancellor is the highest excitement and the ceremony is decorous, in keeping with our more conservative times. It is a very splendid affair but its capacity to give pleasure is reduced with repetition. While Provost I presided with the Chancellor, or one of the Pro-Chancellors, over more than one hundred ceremonies.

Commencements ceremonies date to the very beginning of the College. A very similar event to nowadays was held to mark the admission of the 4th Duke of Bedford as Chancellor in 1768. The new Chancellor presented his portrait by Gainsborough to the College to mark the occasion. It now hangs in the Provost's House. For this occasion music was composed by the Earl of Mornington, the College's first Professor of Music. The ceremony is recorded in detail in Stubbs' History (1889). Happily, in 2007 I received a copy of a letter by a member of the Guinness family written in 1816 (see Appendix 3) which describes the Commencements ceremony at which his degree was conferred. The letter is of great interest because it shows that, even within an event broadly similar to today's, there are significant differences. The detailed dissection of the account will be of considerable interest to historians.

To the more routine events must be added honorary degree ceremonies where degrees, usually doctoral degrees, are awarded to distinguished figures in public life, business, literature and the arts. Commencements for honorary degrees is similar in many respects to that already described, but the Public Orator (Professor John Luce in recent years) delivers a speech in Latin in praise of each candidate. There is usually a formal dinner later in the day where the new doctors are entertained. Some degrees awarded to public figures give rise to a degree of cynicism, but the initiative in the awards comes from the College, not the recipients, and I was never lobbied for an award. A committee to decide on the candidates is chaired by the Chancellor. The committee receives submissions, usually proposed by members of the academic staff, and prepares a list of names to be proposed to the Senate. The Provost may comment on the names proposed but has no formal role in the selection of names. I had a practical rule that degrees should not be awarded to active politicians, but could be awarded after retirement from public life to acknowledge an outstanding and universally acknowledged achievement.

My most memorable honorary degree Commencements was the award of a doctorate to King Juan Carlos of Spain in July 1986. We wanted to recognise his courage and steadfastness in facing down the last attempt of old-regime supporters to suppress the new parliamentary democracy. The King and his Queen, Sofia, were guests in our house as the procession lined up. He had a fine presence and a charming manner. He asked permission to speak at the ceremony and did so in English and Latin. I had introduced him in English, but the Latin tradition was sustained in the oration delivered by John Luce. The ceremony was extensively covered by television in Spain. A friend, on a visit to Barcelona, told me he had been taken by surprise at seeing us on Catalan television. Some other notable figures in Europe's history who received honorary doctorates were Jacques Delors, President of the European Commission, and Alexander Dubček, who led his country's Prague Spring with courage and conviction.

On the occasion of Dublin's Millennium in 1988 we awarded honorary degrees to a group of well-known citizens such as the Lord Mayor, Carmencita Hederman, the television presenter Gay Byrne, Maureen Potter and others. Willie Bermingham, a fireman at Pearse Street Fire Station beside the College, well-known for his charitable work, wore his gown after the ceremony to show his colleagues at the fire station. The lead musician of the Chieftains, Paddy Moloney, was also honoured. I have always enjoyed their music. Our paths have crossed in airports several times since then and he has come to shake hands with me. I appreciate it very much.

The occasion of the Millennium Commencements was one other where we mixed Latin and English and there are other examples, simply to improve communication and understanding of what we were doing. Although very few people now know Latin, even at an elementary level, the continuity of a dignified ceremonial that has lasted for several centuries is still something to uphold.

At an early stage I discovered that no ceremonies existed for the induction of a Chancellor, or for that matter, a Provost. An oath of office is administered by the Provost to the incoming Chancellor, but in what environment and with what audience? There was no tradition I could discover and the outgoing office-holders had been so long in service that there was no memory of what the procedure should be. When Bedell Stanford, the retired Professor of Greek and former Senator in Dáil Éireann, became Chancellor I summoned the Board to assemble in the Library of the Provost's House, gowned, and the new Chancellor read the oath of office before the Board. We helped him into the heavy Chancellor's gown. The two of us were then photographed in the Provost's Garden. A man who liked every dignity and ceremony but also had a sense of humour, he said to me afterwards, 'you have to be a bit pompous to enjoy events like this, but I do confess I liked it'.

The principle was extended later at the induction of my successor Tom Mitchell, Professor of Latin, in 1991. The Board assembled in the Dining Room of the Provost's House, a magnificent room, with period furniture, silver and classical paintings. The oath of office was read in a formal atmosphere. Journalists were present to record the occasion. One of them thanked me for being invited to this ancient ceremony. I could hardly reveal that it had been invented a few weeks earlier. I myself had been admitted to office by reading the oath in an office before the College Secretary. It wasn't enough to mark an important occasion in the College's history. I believe that formality is required when appointments to major offices are made.

A sadder occasion was the funeral of my predecessor, Leland Lyons. Since his retirement Lee had been working on a biography of William Butler Yeats and had access to Yeats family papers. He had been studying Yeats's preoccupation with the occult with much of his time spent in the United States. The work continued on his return to Dublin. He fell ill in the autumn of 1983 and was taken to hospital with severe stomach pains. Examination showed that he was suffering from acute haemorrhagic pancreatitis. The cause was unknown. Unhappily he sank remorselessly over about eight weeks, sinking into unconsciousness towards the end, dying on September 21st, 1983.

The question of how to conduct a funeral arose, but no Provost had died since Alton in 1952 and there was no good record of the details of the funeral. I have been told that, by old tradition, Provost Alton's coffin was carried around Front Square on a low carriage in a procession of College staff and students, a sort of 'beating the bounds' before arriving at the Chapel. Nothing like that was contemplated on this occasion. It was suggested that I should precede the coffin into College Chapel, but I did not want to project myself into the centre of the event; Lee was an active member of the Church of Ireland, used to being preceded to the Chapel by the Mace-Bearer. This stimulated the idea that the Mace-Bearer should precede the coffin which was carried by four volunteers from among the security staff. The mace was covered by black crape. The Chapel was crammed to capacity with, in addition to family members, major figures in public life, academic staff and friends. The funeral service was also relayed to a large group in the Dining Hall. Some time later on St Stephen's Day, a very quiet day in the College, an urn with Lee's ashes was interred privately in the tiny burial ground which adjoins the Chapel. A handful of us were there to witness the event respectfully. He is commemorated by a memorial tablet above the grave.

Lee was a dedicated member of the Church of Ireland and a regular Chapel-goer. I, a rather non-observant Presbyterian, was not. I do, however, respect the dignity of Chapel services and greatly enjoy its excellent choir music. It was my habit to read the Christmas message at the annual carol service and I always read the lesson at the Trinity Monday service. When it fell to me to read the lesson I insisted on the Authorised Version of the Bible because it contains some of the most beautiful literary English ever written. I attended Poppy Day ceremonies in St Patrick's Cathedral. Both my brothers-in-law grew up in Northern Ireland and had served in World War II with distinction, one being awarded a Military Medal. I thought it right to honour them and their fellow soldiers and airmen. I reject as nonsense the idea that to serve in the forces that defeated Hitler's armies was in some way anti-national.

I attended Citizenship Sunday services in Christ Church Cathedral annually and twice read the lesson in Irish which was broadcast on national radio. In a moment of bravado I offered to read and then felt I had been mad to do so. However, I read it over (the Ten Commandments) with one of our Professors of Irish, Gordon Quin, who with one or two corrections passed me as fit. I had to dredge my secondary school knowledge, but I owe my pronunciation to my Irish teacher in St Andrews, Mr Murphy, a native of Cahirciveen, who must have given me the *blas* on which I was complimented by a Supreme Court Judge. I honestly enjoyed learning Irish and much still stays with me but, as with many others, it withers from lack of use or reason to use it.

One of the more remarkable public occasions in which I took part was when I had been asked to lay a foundation brick for St Patrick's Cathedral Grammar School, which was being rebuilt. This was at the invitation of the redoubtable Dean Griffin. Afterwards, it being a Sunday, I was invited to take part in the late afternoon evensong. The ceremony of brick-laying complete, I was ready to go into the Cathedral and he said to me, 'By the way, you're giving the sermon today'. I was totally unprepared, flabbergasted and very concerned about my ability to perform. By good fortune I had read a pamphlet about the Grammar School in preparation for the ceremony there. I spoke about the School and its history and about education. I wished the pupils a good future. It got by, but many more such invitations would have led to early retirement.

10.
CRISES AND FIRES

CRISES

INEVITABLY, THERE WERE
periods of stress and difficulty. One of the worst from my
perspective was a strike by weekly-paid staff which lasted for two
weeks in February and March 1983. The origin of the strike was a
pay claim for parity with workers in Dublin Corporation who had
recently gained a raise. Parity, it was claimed, probably correctly,
had always been granted in the past, but the Fine Gael-led coalition
of the time had budgetary problems and had imposed a wages
stand-still. The axe fell between the Corporation workers and the
College's weekly-paid staff.

All appeals to the Higher Education Authority, the Department
of the Public Service and the Department of Education were
fruitless. They were determined to implement government policy
even if the consequence was the indefinite closure of the University,
something I could not accept. Scenes of both stress and farce
followed, a liberal society not being at its best or most clear-minded
when decisions must be taken. The absence of the weekly-paid staff
who picketed the College meant that the security, cleaning, library
and maintenance staff were on strike. The senior administrative and
maintenance staff with senior academics manned the Library and
the switchboard, opened gates and provided cleaning services.
Gerry and I got up early every morning to vacuum-clean lecture
theatres, clean boards and bag rubbish. There were complex plans

to pass pickets to bring in heating-oil and other necessary materials, but, fortunately, most of the plans never had to be implemented.

Strangely, students were quite unresponsive to the strike. For a small minority, the class war and revolution would soon break out in all of their grim beauty. Most behaved entirely as usual, attending lectures, using the Library, quite untouched. The academic staff were divided between those who supported the policy of keeping the College open, some who thought they should be on strike also and the majority who didn't want to be counted. Some gained fame by giving lectures in pubs. One professor, who profoundly disapproved of what he saw as strike-breaking when Gerry and I cleaned the lecture theatres, was quite prepared to give his lectures as usual in the rooms we had just cleaned after we had left. I still don't see his logic.

As for farce, some revolutionaries decided to sabotage the sewage system of the Arts Building by pouring cement into the lavatories but chose a type of cement which was easy to remove again. Aidan Clarke and Dave Mulhall, our Staff Secretary, and I made frequent visits to the Department of the Public Service. They had no help or useful advice for us. As the strike progressed I held a general meeting of the academic staff to brief them on what was happening. I tried to be moderate and conciliatory in what I said. David Webb joked afterwards that its blandness made him think of Stanley Baldwin addressing Parliament in Westminster during the General Strike of 1926.

The strike ended after two weeks. We had no option if the University was to stay open because those who provided service were overstretched and tired. We finished on one day in the College Secretary's office. The Secretary, Gerry Giltrap, stood loyally by. At one point he held two telephones: one to the Union, one to the Department of the Public Service. I remember his telling the Department that, if they had a good idea about how to settle the strike, it would be timely right now because we were in the process of settling with the Union. Squawks of disapproval could be heard. An enraged Minister for Education, Dick Burke, fined the College £100,000 for ignoring a government directive. I never accepted it.

It was finally reversed by Gemma Hussey when she became Minister. I owe her thanks.

In retrospect I was probably naïve on questions of industrial relations. I suppose we could have closed the College and blamed the Government for prolonging the strike by its intransigence but my motivation was always to keep the College open. I discussed it with Professor Charles McCarthy, a man with much experience of industrial relations. I told him I would have resigned as Provost if the situation had got worse. He said that nobody should resign over a strike, the issues never called for it. I couldn't help thinking that some of the women cleaners on the picket stood to gain less than £1 a week if the strike was successful and that the only ones who would not lose money or sleep were the trade union officials and the civil servants. After the strike ended and the dust settled life returned to normal very quickly. It left few scars, but I had an uneasy feeling that things could have gone awfully wrong.

TRINITY WEEK
AND THE BALL

The high point of Trinity Week socially was the Ball, an occasion of many headaches for the administration. It was very popular. Tickets were in great demand with up to 5,000 attending. It must have been a great joy to insurers whose costs were very high, which fact almost closed the Ball on several occasions. The potential for trouble was large, but nothing very serious ever happened apart from scenes of hedonism with much too much drinking.

For our first few years in the Provost's House gate-crashing was a real nuisance with athletic young men climbing over the boundary railings, quite a feat. On one occasion as we returned to the House a gate-crasher who had climbed into the Stable Yard was attempting to climb a second wall into the garden at the back of the House. He lost his footing and fell through the roof of our greenhouse with a resounding crash, then stood up and smashed his way out through the side. Gerry was furious and all set to grab him, but I held her back, not knowing how drunk or violent this Tarzan was. Apparently uninjured, he left the demolished greenhouse behind and climbed out to Nassau Street once more. I heard nothing more of him nor ever discovered who he was, but surely God must extend his special protection to people like him.

On one Ball evening I was changing into my dinner jacket when Dave Mulhall phoned me to come to Front Gate at once. There was 'terrible trouble'. Dave was one of the organisers of the Ball. I went down to find that the Security Staff had gone on a lightning strike. Half of the Ball-goers were inside the College, the rest were locked out, not pleased, and some of them were banging on Front Gate with bottles. It was an exceptionally hot evening. The atmosphere was not improved by a car going on fire outside the College from an engine fault. I marched into this daunting scene knowing I had to do something but not sure what.

I walked to the group of strikers who were waving placards and asked for a spokesman. The two of us went into a side room where I learned that the problem was with guard dogs which patrolled the College walls to deter gate-crashers. The security men thought the dogs were to be used in the Ball area. I explained that was not intended and that the dogs would only be used in College Park which was isolated from the Ball area by locked gates. Someone had said the dogs came from Northern Ireland; in fact, they came from a security firm in the north city. The spokesman said he had heard enough and called on his colleagues to go back to work, which they did with no worries. College gates were opened, the revellers passed in, and the Ball went on as usual. I heard no more about it and ruled out any penalties. I assured those who assumed I had given money to get the strikers to go back that they didn't know much about me. An ugly scene had passed; life went on.

For about twenty years the College had become familiar with sit-ins but after the departure of Joe Duffy, who combined aggressive behaviour with a keen sense for publicity, it had all sunk to a low level and is now almost unknown. Arguments about medical cards led to an occupation of some government offices and the arrest of several students who were sent to jail until they purged their contempt of court. I was asked to intervene on their behalf but declined on the grounds that they had made a free choice on what they thought was a serious issue of principle. It was for them to take legal advice before they next appeared in court. They apologised and were discharged.

Inside College a relatively serious sit-in took place in the Director of Buildings Office. Students occupied the Office beside the College Chapel for ten days and locked themselves in. They climbed on the roof of the building. They could have damaged or destroyed important documents and plans of the College's building programme. I did not think this would be done maliciously but it could have been done by carelessness. We assigned four security men to keep watch on the premises, mostly because of fear of a fall from the roof.

After a few days we told the student leaders that they would receive a daily cumulative bill for the services of the security men. At first they treated this as a joke, but weakened as the bill increased. A few days later we received a message asking that the number of security staff be reduced to two. We knew then that the end was in sight and the sit-in was abandoned shortly afterwards. I fined the Student's Union £15,000. Some people thought this excessive, but it was less than the actual cost to the College. I also had the advantage of knowing that the Union was surprisingly wealthy and, at worst, it would have to cancel a disco or some other such event. Much to my surprise the fine was accepted without discussion and the valuable principle established that sit-ins, no matter how sincerely intended, had costs which should be kept in mind. Demos and sit-ins are now pale shadows of what they used to be. Perhaps different economic circumstances will change things again but, for the present, students seem generally conservative in outlook, more interested in a mix of hard work and a good time than wanting to change the world.

A very traumatic event took place on 17th May 1974 while I was still Senior Lecturer. I was about to drive home with my son Niall and a friend from the car park beside the Botany Department. There was a loud bang. Instinctively I knew it was a bomb. I left the boys and went to see what had happened. A car-bomb had exploded outside the College in South Leinster Street near the bottom of Kildare Street. Tragically, three young women, secretaries on their way home from work, were killed. The car's radiator and parts of the engine were blown over the roof of the Moyne Institute to land in the middle of College Park. The Moyne Institute was protected by Trinity's stout granite wall which was pock-marked by bomb debris. A lecture organised by Professor Louis Cullen was being given in the Moyne's lecture theatre. Fortunately a slide projector was being used and curtains were drawn which received glass fragments as the windows came in. There were no serious injuries inside College.

As a College Officer I went to see what I could do. People had dispersed quickly and the place was deserted. The door to the Moyne was open and there was a thin trail of blood along the hall and down the stairs. Afterwards I discovered that the blood came from a student who had jerked and banged his head as the bomb exploded. He was using an unfamiliar piece of equipment which he had switched on at the moment of the explosion. In the shock and confusion he went home believing that he had caused the bang himself and only woke to reality when he heard what had really happened later.

I telephoned John Walsh, the Agent, a retired British Army man, who was responsible for the College's buildings. He arranged for replacement glass immediately, commenting realistically that he had best be first in the queue. The bombing, one of three in Dublin on that horrific day, took place at evening rush-hour and caused traffic chaos. My colleague Brian Spencer, Professor of Biochemistry, who had some medical background, tried to aid the victims, but they were beyond help. Some slightly injured people came into Trinity through the pedestrian gate beside the Moyne and were taken to Sir Patrick Dun's Hospital, the only one accessible because of the traffic conditions, though it was not an accident and emergency hospital.

FIRES

Gerry and I were two days from the end of our 1984 summer holiday in Switzerland when Gerry Giltrap was on the phone to tell me that there had been a serious fire in College and that the Dining Hall had been severely damaged. It had happened on July 14th. He assured me that the fire had been extinguished and that our insurance cover was satisfactory. Arrangements had already been made to start reconstruction and Cramptons, a distinguished firm of builders in Dublin, had been appointed to manage the restoration programme, which would involve numerous specialist skills. We decided to complete our holiday. Should I have come back to show concern even if I had no specific role to play? I really don't know.

The fire had broken out in the Dining Hall in the evening, probably started in the small bell tower where the bell for Commons was rung. It got into the roof space above the plaster ceiling of the Hall. The huge horizontal timbers and the rafters of the 200 year old building caught fire and flames leaped up through the roof until it collapsed. The adjoining Common Room was also destroyed. As the fire broke out a relay of College people carried out portraits from the Common Room but the large portraits in the Dining Hall were far too heavy to move. There was water damage. Later, safety officers from the Corporation decided that the brick chimney which separated the Common Room from the Dining Hall was now unsafe and should come down. The work was started brick by brick but, somewhere in the process and fortunately without injury, a large mass of brickwork became unstable and crashed through the floor of the Dining Hall as effectively as a large bomb. All this had to be put right.

There has been much interest in the fire and its cause. The simple fact is that nothing has ever emerged. The Gardaí looked at the case of an arsonist who had recently been discharged from prison but there did not appear to be any connection. The possibility that the fire had been started accidentally by a dosser sleeping rough and finding shelter in the bell-tower past whatever security was in force can't be dismissed, but there really is no significant evidence.

The refurbishment of the Dining Hall was then, of course, full of interest. The great portraits survived miraculously, covered with soot and ashes with some damage to the more ornate frames. They were taken down, cleaned and restored. One bishop lost a foot to the flames, another dignitary part of his gown, but their restoration was not a great challenge. The very large portrait of Frederick Prince of Wales by Thomas Hudson which hangs over the Dining Hall door survived and only needed cleaning but its superb frame by the French carver Paul Petit was damaged by falling debris and some projecting parts broken off. It was magnificently restored by Mary McGrath and Susan Mulhall and re-gilded to its present splendour. Frederick was elected Chancellor to the University in 1728. He never visited Ireland but the portrait was his gift to Trinity in recognition of his appointment. He pre-deceased his father George II.

The ornate but simple plaster-work of the ceiling was restored to identical form with its predecessor by using large chunks of fallen plaster as templates and re-casting them. The Hall's wooden panelling was cleaned and, where necessary, restored. The parquet floor of the Hall was taken away and the original stone floor restored. All of the furniture was replaced — large tables and many stout chairs. A whole community in County Cork was kept busy for over a month making chairs, in fact the whole project gave a great deal of work to skilled craftsmen throughout the country. They deserve great praise. The ceiling is now held up by steel girders as is the floor of the Common Room. I do not think that a returning graduate today, who did not know of the fire, would notice any difference. The fire and the work of restoration were recorded on film by Al Byrne, a graduate of the College. Al has recently donated his films of this and other College events to the College Library archives. The 'fire' film captures events and emotions that will soon be fading from memory.

Afterwards the College commissioned the architectural firm of de Blacam and Meagher (Shane de Blacam and John Meagher) to restore the long high room on the west side of the Dining Hall which also had been damaged. This was the original kitchen for the Dining Hall with great stone fireplaces. It was still in use when I was an undergraduate. It was plain, gloomy and rather depressing, extending to the full height of the Dining Hall without intermediate floors. Even in an overcrowded College it had not found anyone to take a serious interest in it. de Blacam and Meagher transformed this into the Atrium, still an open space from the floor to ceiling but now surrounded by balconies, beautifully panelled in beech wood. It has become a favourite place for College receptions. It was used for the launch of the College's Quatercentenary programme. In addition, the Common Room was restored in detail including its ornate chandelier which had been crushed by falling debris. Off the Common Room a bar was created, an exact imitation of the Kaerntner Bar, an Art Nouveau bar in Vienna, a fine *jeu d'esprit* to complete our work.

The fire was the first of several over the next six months. On one occasion the Players' Theatre in House Number 3 in Front Square was the source of smoke that infiltrated neighbouring buildings including the Provost's Office where I was working at the time. The smoke was caused by fire in the seat of a vinyl-covered armchair in the basement under the Theatre. It was easily extinguished. This fire was a major stimulus to the construction of a new theatre because Players' with its stored costumes and flats was now revealed as a serious fire hazard.

A similar fire took place in the basement of the Museum Building where, again, a vinyl plastic armchair provided much smoke. It was becoming clear that arson was involved. Gerry Giltrap had a saying that once is happenstance, twice coincidence, three times is enemy action. The next fire took place in the Classical Society's rooms, then at the top of House 6. Again it was easily put out, but this time it was clear that papers and books had been gathered into a pile and set alight. Again the fire was put out without much difficulty.

The last, a serious fire, took place in December of that year. Gerry and I had attended the staff Christmas Dinner early in the evening together with former Provost McConnell and Mrs McConnell. As we left the dinner at about 11 o'clock we saw that a fire had broken out on the top floor of East Chapel, a range of rooms and offices forming the east wing of the Chapel through three stories. The fire had started in the Cumann Gaelach (Irish Society) rooms in a tin waste-paper bin. It could have been caused by a discarded cigarette. On the Giltrap principle it was, I think, more probably arson.

The wing was substantially damaged and had to be refurbished. At the height of the fire I went into the Chapel to try to assess the damage. I could see flames through windows high on the Chapel Wall and hear the cracking of glass and slates from the heat of the fire. Smoke made a wet handkerchief over my nose and mouth necessary while water flowed down the wall from the Fire Brigade's hoses. Fortunately the Chapel suffered only minor damage from smoke and water. The next day I asked the Catholic Chaplain if he felt he should approach St Andrew's Church in Westland Row for access while the Chapel was refurbished as far as was necessary. He replied that the Chapel was still usable, so normality was resumed in a still soggy and smoke-smelling Chapel without a hiatus. I salute his clarity and determination on the occasion.

After this rather frightening six months of fires there were no more during my period in office. The person or persons responsible have never been found. It is not certain that all the fires were caused by one person, but it seems clear that some, or even all, were malicious, arson in fact, and frighteningly dangerous in an institution used and lived in by many people, with a rich architectural and cultural heritage to protect. My best guess is that the last four fires were somebody's malicious idea of fun. The Chapel fire revealed the damage that could be caused by a fire extending from one source in a single room. Perhaps the perpetrator, scared by his success, gave up at that point. About the first, or really, about all the fires, I just don't know who was responsible or even a likely candidate.

In my time a problem which had troubled my predecessors abated. This was drug taking, involving injection by hypodermic needles, usually in lavatories of student rooms which in many cases were outside the rooms at the bottom of staircases. The discarded needles were a depressing sight. As a city-centre institution the drug-takers may have come in from city streets and might have involved some students, but there was little evidence of this. Better security systems and the provision of locked doors for staircases that were historically open, probably played a major part in reducing the problem.

I am opposed to all drug-taking; it is socially undesirable and, above all, illegal. I invited Gardaí from Pearse Street to come into College to advise us about any measures we should take. Several senior Gardaí came. Their advice, very welcome to me, was that drugs were not a problem in Trinity at the time. We had good relationships with the Garda, who helped us on several occasions. Once when we had had a rash of small break-ins and thefts, some plain-clothes Gardaí stationed themselves in the College for a few weeks. They noticed a few people already known to them, approached them and congratulated them on their new-found dedication to University education. The thefts stopped.

11.
'EDIFICE COMPLEX'

WHEN I WAS PROVOST, Shane de Blacam, one of the architects of the Atrium development of the Dining Hall and subsequently of the Beckett Theatre, said I had an 'edifice complex'. It was probably not the first use of the joke, but I enjoyed it. I came to an interest in buildings and architecture perforce, because the College needed to make decisions about how to develop its site. Numbers were climbing slowly in the sixties, but already the pressure of students was forcing us to make an inventory of our teaching spaces and to decide on priorities for modification of existing buildings and development of new ones.

As Dean of Science and as Senior Lecturer I gained experience of these problems. Several of our older buildings were reconstructed internally. The old anatomy lecture theatre, which was little used, gave way to our first science library and to a lecture theatre. The Dixon Hall, built in memory of A. F. Dixon ('Anatomy Dick' to distinguish him from his brother H. H. Dixon, Professor of Botany, 'Botany Dick') was originally used for public lectures, but more for student dances, 'hops' as they were called in those days. It had fallen into disuse. It was rebuilt internally to provide laboratory and office space on two floors for the Physics Department and has since been replaced by the Sami Nasr Building, a large modern laboratory building, which commemorates the beneficence of Sami Nasr, a refugee from Middle Eastern troubles, who became a graduate student in palaeontology under the guidance of R. G. S. Hudson, FRS, then head of the Department of Geology. He obtained a master's degree and went on to a very successful career in oil exploration, becoming wealthy in the process. He married an Irish wife, who reminded him of his time in Trinity, with which he had kept in contact. He had retired to Australia, where I made contact with him. I suggested that he might consider funding research in new materials in the Department of Physics to which he agreed.

I was Senior Lecturer towards the end of Provost McConnell's long period in office. I discovered that the use of the Examination Hall was formally the prerogative of the Senior Lecturer and that it was included in the list of lecture theatres. I persuaded the College that it had become shabby, as indeed it had, and must be redecorated. The College formed a committee for the purpose, which came to be known as the Committee on Taste (I still cringe at the title) consisting of the Agent (John Walsh), Anne Crookshank, who later became Professor of the History of Art, and myself. The Agent was responsible for the management and construction of buildings; later the title Director of Buildings was used. We had some advice from distinguished specialists, initially Raymond McGrath from the Office of Public Works, but mostly we made up our own minds. It was great fun. Anne, as the person with the most real professional knowledge, gave much of the leadership. She climbed up scaffolding to look at the minute details of plaster and paintwork. 'More gold' she would cry as we thought the gilding too dull.

At that time, prior to the opening of the National Concert Hall, the Examination Hall was used by smaller orchestras. On one such occasion the newly decorated Hall was seen by the public for the first time. The effect was stunningly beautiful. Our Committee moved on to the College Chapel and removed the black tarry resin that had disfigured the Chapel for generations and restored the lighter colours of the wooden pews. We resisted suggestions from the clergy that the Chapel would be better served by re-arranging the pews to face the altar for it would have abandoned the original arrangement which provided for a preacher who might address the congregation from a raised pulpit in the middle of the Chapel. The original pulpit is still there at one side of the Chapel but divorced from its supporting plinth which is now used as a lectern.

We found other tasks for our committee. Lights and illuminations were always a testing and contentious problem both in the Chapel and the Examination Hall. There were conflicting views about what constituted good taste in the type of lighting and lampshades to be used. They had to be talked through and, of course, there was an overriding need to be able to see books and music properly. The great chandelier in the Examination Hall, a magnificent piece from the pre-Union House of Lords, could not be used with candles for reasons of safety.

During Leland Lyons' time the Arts and Social Sciences building had been completed and was opened in 1978 by President Patrick Hillery. Rooms previously used for Arts Departments which migrated to the new building became student residences. Number 35 in New Square had housed the School of Modern Languages with the Departments of French and German and their libraries. I had been taught there as an undergraduate. Samuel Beckett lectured there before his precipitate pre-war departure from College. Leland also initiated the building of the Sports Hall (Luce Hall) at the back of College. It provided for his favourite sport, squash, in which he had played at international level, and which he continued to play there while Provost. Many other sporting activities were also housed there. It fell to me as Provost to open the Hall after Leland's retirement when he was in North America. It was one of my first social appearances together with Martin O'Donoghue, then Minister for Education. Some government activity had aroused student wrath. Eggs were thrown, I don't know at which of us, but one smashed on the lapel of Martin's splendid overcoat. He was not pleased.

While Senior Lecturer I had become involved as College spokesman in a number of planning issues. The first was the Arts and Social Sciences Building. The College's plans, prepared by the architect Paul Koralek, were appealed against by several colleagues and private persons concerned with conservation of the city's buildings and streetscape. College was represented at the planning hearing by Eamonn Walsh SC, a very able lawyer, with that most desirable of characteristics, a record of success in planning appeal hearings. I listened with some anxiety as my colleagues condemned forthrightly what they saw as the ugliness of the planned building. I asked Eamonn Walsh who had remained impassive through all this whether we should not reply to these seemingly important points. He answered that the Planning and Development Act was not concerned with whether buildings were beautiful or ugly and that the Planning Inspector would not take these considerations into account. Now if criticism had been directed at the adequacy of the drains, for example, there would have been much more cause to reply. We obtained approval in due course with the proviso that the building be moved a few metres farther away from the Nassau Street frontage than had been planned and that trees along the wall should be protected.

Later, in 1974, I was again a spokesman for College at a hearing in City Hall where we sought to obtain a Compulsory Purchase Order (CPO) for houses on College's east perimeter on Westland Row. The College Board had adopted the farsighted policy of purchasing all buildings on Trinity's island site and had been picking them up as they came on the market. We owned all but three or four houses on our Westland Row frontage and now our case for expansion was driven by increasing pressure of student numbers. The CPO was supported by the Corporation and the opposition from a number of small businesses and professional offices was not very strong, mainly concerned, I think, with the adequacy of compensation. The CPO was granted and, in the outcome, the Westland Row buildings were refurbished as offices or small laboratories which opened through a large roofed open space into the new Hamilton Building. It has several large lecture theatres, a much enlarged science library and several laboratory-based departments. The architect was Ronnie Tallon of Scott, Tallon and Walker.

My experience of planning procedures proved useful as we developed our site. Already we had considered a major development of buildings at College's East End. Brian Spencer, Professor of Biochemistry and Dean of Science and I, as Senior Lecturer, travelled to the United States to help us evolve ideas for our site. We visited Stanford University near San Francisco, the University of Southern California in Los Angeles and Dartmouth College in New Hampshire. We looked at laboratory design and teaching arrangements particularly for medicine. Dartmouth, about the same size as Trinity and with more limited resources than the other two relative giants, was very instructive.

At the end of our tour we sat down in a motel somewhere in snow-covered New England and wrote our report for College. This was the genesis of our East End Plan which established a principle that new building should be guided by a master plan for the College's physical development. The broad idea was generally accepted by our colleagues but little of it was actually implemented and a more pragmatic approach was used which took account of needs as they arose and resources as they became available. The driving force was usually student numbers so that plans constantly had to be revised upward in scale. It is difficult to think now that Sir Myles Wright, a distinguished planner, advised that our site should be planned for 6,000 students. We now have 15,300 of whom a minority are off-site, especially medical and nursing students.

When I became Provost in 1981 I did not have any very specific building plans. We had some capital, but not a very large amount, and it was kept for a rainy day. I was conscious of the need to improve sub-standard accommodation as a first priority. I tried to clear up a couple of Augean Stables — the basement of the Physiology Department still contained College library books in a very poor dust-laden environment. They were consolidated with the main collections. The basement of the Chapel had a huge map collection (half a million items) spread over a large stone floor area in great disarray. We created a Map Library in part of the old gym now freed by the construction of the Luce Hall and appointed a Map Librarian. Now maps were suitably stored and could be consulted. There were also book repositories to be built at our

Sports Field in Santry. The enormous annual influx of books could not be accommodated in College, so several blocks had been built in Santry as book stores, two in my time. A service to transport books to and from College was already established before 1981.

Leland Lyons had instituted a fund-raising committee but on retirement, he wrote letters of thanks to its members and dissolved it. This left me to make a new start. After a settling-in period as Provost, I began to develop more ambitious ideas for building. It occurred to me that the College's fourth centenary in 1992 would be a good focus for a fund-raising and building campaign. I established an objective that there should be a significant building each, for Science and for Arts. I had been in the habit of visiting departments and hearing their problems. I visited the Computer Science Department housed in Pearse Street. It was already successful and very attractive to students, rapidly becoming our biggest department. I was appalled at the very poor quality of the rooms and at the ceilings which flaked plaster on to the computers. I made it my first choice.

On a visit to the US I called on Tony (now Sir Anthony) O'Reilly, Chief Executive of the Heinz Corporation, at his offices in Pittsburgh to seek his support. We talked at first about sport, especially rugby, remembering school and international games. I had discovered that his father had attended Trinity as a solicitors' apprentice student. I asked him to support a building named for his parents and dedicated to communications technology. I said that I would put £1 million on the table if he would put his £1 million beside it. He agreed to think about it and, a little later, confirmed that he would provide the gift. This created quite a sensation when it was announced. *The Irish Times* had a leading article which praised the donor's generosity and imagination. It was a first of its kind and made the academic world in Ireland realise what could be accomplished. Much larger sums are spent in our universities now for building programmes, but £2 million was a substantial sum in the cash-starved mid-eighties. When the O'Reilly Institute was opened in February 1989 we had a fine ceremony and lunch afterwards in the Examination Hall with complimentary speeches.

It was a wonderful occasion.

Our second Quatercentenary project came in Arts. I knew that students of Drama and Theatre Studies were miserably housed and that plays were being performed in rooms around the periphery of the campus that were uncomfortable and in winter very inadequately heated. We had to do better or get out of the subject. Barbara Wright was an enthusiastic lobbyist for a theatre project. At the same time the re-housing of Players from Number 3 College seemed to me to be urgent. Players' Theatre had been revealed as a fire hazard by the arsonist.

I had had some contact with Coca Cola in Atlanta. The Corporation's President, Donald Keough, had shown an interest in theatre in Ireland where his family roots were. The Secretary of the Corporation was also friendly. I discovered that Coca Cola would provide capital for a Chair in Drama and Theatre Studies but it was not policy to support building projects. I decided that we should use College capital to build a theatre, given that we could at least see how to staff the Department, and obtained Board assent. Afterwards there was some puzzlement about the level of consultation involved and I was told that nobody knew who had decided to build a theatre. In fact it was largely a personal decision of my own. The architects were again de Blacam and Meagher. The theatre is at the entry to College Park from New Square. There was some conflict about the re-location of Players who preferred their familiar old premises to the new ones on offer, but the safety issue was overriding.

During the building of the theatre in 1986 I paid a visit to Sam Beckett in Paris. As far as I knew he had not maintained contacts in Trinity other than with A. J.(Con) Leventhal who also left to join him in Paris after the war years. Beckett had gone to Paris as a lecturer at the École Normale Supérieure. He returned to Trinity as a lecturer in French in 1930 for a brief period when, apparently finding his career utterly dispiriting, he left a little over a year later to live on the continent. He finally settled in Paris after the war. He was awarded the Nobel Prize in 1969. I was driven more by curiosity than anything else in my desire to meet him. I had thought that I should attempt to secure some manuscript material for the Library but quickly dismissed it as an idea knowing that other universities had already begun Beckett collections. I decided to ask him if we might ask his permission to name our new theatre, then under construction, in his honour.

The meeting was arranged in a rather cloak-and-dagger manner. One contacted his publisher who would indicate his availability or not and tell when and where to find him. I arrived at a bar, modern in style with much chromium. I sat down, ordered some coffee and suddenly a door opened at the back of the bar and he emerged, as I had seen him in many photographs, dressed in a heavy fisherman-type sweater. We talked for about an hour over coffee. He began by saying that he owed Trinity an apology for his sudden departure, so sudden it seems that he hadn't returned his room keys. I said I didn't think anybody would mind very much today.

He asked me about Trinity. I was forced to realise that he had left more than fifty years before, when he asked me about the College he remembered as a young man. College Officers and staff of his time were nearly all only names to me with little resonance, only one or two in medicine being names I recognised. He had been a very active sportsman in his youth at Portora Royal School and as a student in Trinity. He talked mostly about cricket and about rugby. I asked for permission to use his name, which he gave without hesitation. One of my strongest recollections is his accent. He came of a middle class Protestant family who lived in Foxrock, a suburb for the decidedly well-to-do, then and now. His accent was the distinctive one of the Dublin middle-classes which he had not lost in spite of his long residence in France and his deep immersion in French language and culture. I found him gentle, friendly and likeable, our meeting a fine outcome to my slightly quixotic journey.

Other buildings followed. As I recorded earlier we added a new block of student residences on the Pearse Street frontage which incorporated the student health service and an upgraded day-nursery for pre-school children of staff and students. I have already referred to the Hamilton Building, named in honour of the extremely distinguished graduate, William Rowan Hamilton, the mathematician who formulated the theory of quaternions. Construction began towards the end of my Provostship. It was opened in 1992. The funding was greatly assisted by Michael Smith, TD, at that time Minster with responsibility for Science. He was approachable and friendly, sought no recognition of any kind for himself, and deserves our thanks.

The Moyne Institute was expanded considerably in the late eighties and early nineties. The Institute, which houses the Department of Microbiology, was founded by Lady Grania Guinness and members of her family to honour her father, Lord Moyne, who had been assassinated by Stern Gang terrorists in Egypt where he was British Minister Resident. The Institute had grown considerably under the vigorous leadership of Professor John Arbuthnott and had developed important lines of research. It had become too small and we had reluctantly decided that microbiology should be re-housed elsewhere.

John Arbuthnott and I had the delicate task of discussing this matter with Lady Grania who, after her marriage, had the title Grania, Marchioness of Normanby. She had retained an interest in the Institute and in Ireland throughout her life, and she had become Pro-Chancellor at my invitation. Her reply to our unwelcome news was to take the matter into her own hands and she suggested that her family foundation could contribute towards extending the existing building. After some false starts Arthur Gibney was appointed architect. He achieved a very satisfactory expansion at ground level towards the playing-fields in College Park. This greatly increased the laboratory and research space. This is the place to record our gratitude to this very able, friendly and, in a good way, forceful woman. I delight that her interest extended to receiving the Moyne's publications, and to the surprise of the academic staff, reading them and asking pertinent questions.

Lady Normanby's home is in Whitby in Yorkshire, the home port of Captain James Cook who explored, mapped and made scientific observations in Hawaii, Tahiti, Australia and New Zealand. He is commemorated in Whitby's museum. Trinity College Dublin had

139

received as a gift a considerable treasure of weapons and other artefacts dating from Cook's fateful visit to Hawaii. They were placed in the care of the National Museum in 1882 and 1894. The details are recorded in K. C. Bailey's History. Lady Normanby negotiated with Dr Michael Ryan, Keeper of Irish Antiquities in the National Museum and subsequently President of the Royal Irish Academy, to arrange a loan of some of the artefacts for display in Whitby.

Arthur Gibney was also architect for the modification of College's Old Library to provide a better display area for the Book of Kells and for special exhibitions. Originally the Library had open space at ground level in a style similar to the Library at Trinity College Cambridge today. It was enclosed to use for book stacks in the nineteenth century (1891) as the Library expanded its holding and storage space became a headache. The new arrangements would provide for the enormous number of tourists (300,000 annually) who make Trinity one of Ireland's most visited places. The Library is now entered by a door in its south centre. The visitor enters a bookshop first, then to a large room at the east end, where the College's great manuscript treasures, the Book of Kells and the Book of Durrow, are displayed with rich explanatory panels. The quality of the presentation and the splendid manuscripts make a deep impression. On leaving the Treasury, steps lead upstairs and the visitor enters the Long Room where the unique mediaeval Brian Boru Harp, the symbolic harp of Ireland, is to be seen. The visitor descends from the Long Room by a staircase in the middle of the room which leads back to the bookshop and out.

Personally, I remember the old Long Room with some regret. Particularly on a winter evening as darkness approached and few or no tourists were present, the Long Room, silent, reserved, with great book stacks only accessible by high ladders, lined by marble busts, including the famous one of Swift by Roubiliac, is a place of great dignity and remoteness in which the visitor can feel very insignificant. It is to Arthur Gibney's credit that he skilfully achieved the many small and some greater modifications to the Library that we see today. The structural changes serve the ever-pressing needs of tourists and, of course, yield a substantial income used for the Library's needs, but there was a balance to be struck between that and the Library's professional needs. Half of the ground-floor space was dedicated to housing and conservation of manuscript collections.

The high profile of the Book of Kells and of the Book of Durrow may cause one to overlook the very great wealth of the Library's holdings in manuscripts and early printed books. *Treasures of the Library* (1986) edited by the then Librarian, Peter Fox, provides an excellent overview of the collections. John Scattergood's *Manuscripts and Ghosts* (2006) gives an insight into the research possibilities of lesser manuscripts of medieval and Renaissance age. As has been typical of Trinity in the last fifty years the Library too evolves constantly. My successor, Tom Mitchell, initiated the building of the magnificent new James Ussher Library, opened by President Mary McAleese on 11th April 2003, which incidentally includes the Map Library, now the Glucksman Map Library. After another migration, there is stability and we have improved facilities which will see us through the immediate future when the problems of an evolving library can be evaluated in detachment once more.

12.
THE PROVOST'S HOUSE

THE PROVOST'S HOUSE IS No. 1 Grafton Street. An astonishing number of people don't recognise the grey classical building set back from the street in its own grounds, bounded by Lower Grafton Street and Nassau Street. Taxi-drivers would insist that no such building existed or that the gates to the House were permanently closed. People were even known to ring the front door-bell to ask us to settle a bet, whether it was No. 1 Grafton Street or not. The House is a Palladian mansion built for Provost Francis Andrews and completed in 1761. It has been lived in by successive Provosts ever since, the longest such continuous record of residence in a great private house known in Ireland. Andrews was a cosmopolitan figure moving in high social circles and widely travelled. He succeeded the more austere Provost Richard Baldwin in 1758. Baldwin had been Provost for over forty years and had lived to a great age. Most of the classical buildings in Trinity's front area were completed during the provostships of these two men.

The House has a spacious entrance hall. It contains a great wooden chest with padlocks, supposedly once the *cista communis* (common chest) of the College where valuables such as silver plate were stored. Its age is unknown, but probably contemporary with the early days of the House. The earliest records speak of 'The Trunk' which contained the College's silver. The general financial resource of the College is still referred to as the *cista communis.* On the chest sits the Visitors' Book which records the signatures of many distinguished visitors to the House. Several rooms are magnificent showpieces with beautiful plasterwork, silver, and furniture dating to the beginning of the House.

There is a collection of twenty classical paintings bequeathed to the College by Samuel Madden in his will of 1761. The paintings do not include great masterpieces but there are several important portraits in this collection and others acquired by the College at about the same time. There is a portrait of Edmund Burke (1771) by James Barry in the small dining room and 'Coriolanus receiving the Embassy' by Peter Lastman (1625), Rembrandt's mentor, in the Large Dining Room. In the Saloon there is a portrait of Provost Andrews by Anton von Maron, probably painted during a visit to Rome. This portrait faces John Russell, Fourth Duke of Bedford, by Gainsborough, Chancellor in Andrews' time and a personal friend. The Saloon is the greatest room in the House, occupying its full length and overlooking Grafton Street on the first floor. It has excellent plaster and woodwork with further portraits and fine marble busts. It has a high ceiling reaching to the roof of the House. Its size and magnificence made it the main focus for receptions, retirement ceremonies for staff members and, above all in our recollection, for music.

We encouraged music in the House which is very suitable in style for baroque and classical music with small groups or soloists. We began with John O'Conor who played Beethoven, Field and Chopin. We had been very nervous about it, fearing noise from Grafton Street traffic. We worried about the Yamaha grand piano brought in for the occasion, anything larger being physically impossible to get into the room. John was willing to perform after being alerted to possible difficulties. The result was a magical summer evening with wonderful music and the House scented by flowers. We learned a few things to look out for: a ringing telephone in the depths of the House and a striking clock which struck nine just as the twelve notes of Field's 'Minuit' were being played.

We tried to make the House widely available to College visitors. Many music students and staff members came to our concerts. We could seat an audience of fifty. Guests were never charged because we wanted to have complete freedom about who we admitted and did not want to give rights or entitlements which might emerge from ticketed events. Many groups from the city visited us. We began with an invitation to all our neighbours from our road in Stillorgan and proceeded with official visitors to the College, architects with a professional interest in the House and a host of others. Eddie McParland, a distinguished architectural historian and Fellow of the College, presented the House to the professionals; Gerry and I looked after the amateurs and our guests. We consoled ourselves with the thought that we could become tour guides when we retired! There were weeks in which we, Gerry more often than I, showed the House to groups on each of three days. It was very good public relations for the College but it amounted to a lot of work, sometimes tiring because of its sheer volume.

Dinners, lunches, buffet suppers and receptions were all part of our routine. Very often these had the purpose of conducting College business, entertaining College staff, friends and benefactors. We gave a lunch for the Governors of the National Gallery of which I had been an *ex officio* member when President of the Royal Irish Academy. The purpose was largely social but it was an opportunity to have the House's paintings seen by well-informed colleagues.

The House was also used for practical business connected with the College. Weekly meetings of the Annual Officers and Deans, which I thought of as the College's cabinet, took place in its Library. The Finance Committee also met there. I was Chairman of the Central Council of the Dublin Voluntary Hospitals (the seven hospitals associated with Trinity) for most of my time as Provost. Frequent meetings for hospitals' business were also held. The Board of the College meets in a room which is a wing of the House. The Boardroom and the House are approached from the College by a curved passageway, 'The Tunnel', which emerges into Front Square by the door of House Number 1. Processions for degree-conferring ceremonies assembled in the House and Tunnel before emerging into Front Square on their way to the Examination Hall.

The Provost and his family live in the House. Bedrooms and a small dining-room and kitchen are on two upper floors overlooking the College. The first floor bedrooms, the Blue Room and the Green Room are on the same level as the Saloon. Privacy and security during visits present some, but, in our case, no serious problems although occasional intruders arriving when guests were numerous had to be escorted out again. A one-storey extension of the House towards Nassau Street contains a large kitchen, the staff quarters and the Garden Room, a pleasant day room opening on to the garden. The kitchen was used to prepare meals for dinners in either of the formal dining-rooms. We used outside caterers who took over the kitchen for the occasion, anything else would have imposed impossible burdens.

I am old enough to have had some reason to call on Provost Alton in the early fifties, probably in connection with my Scholarship. The Tunnel door to the House was opened by the last butler to serve there. Later there was a Lady Housekeeper who organised meals and the practical details of the household. All this has been swept away. In our time Dick Loane, the Provost's Steward, carried out all the small details of coffee-making, door-opening and telephone answering. Dick, a thoroughly nice, good-humoured and always obliging man was deservedly popular. We still keep in touch. There were also women housekeeping staff among whom we specially remember Frances McGurk who laundered and ironed for us. Gerry cooked family meals and the family, often just the two of us, were the only occupants of the House in the evenings and at weekends. We celebrated Christmas in the House with the family, once made memorable by Brendan Kennelly's company.

VISITS, VISITORS AND GUESTS

The House was the focus for many visits by Heads of State and distinguished public servants from many countries. We assisted the Department of Foreign Affairs in providing hospitality to its visitors. Peter Barry, Minister in the Coalition Government of 1982–85, was a particularly assiduous visitor but Fianna Fáil ministers showed much the same interest. The visits were too numerous to discuss them all, but some were specially memorable.

Crown Prince Akihito and Crown Princess Michiko of Japan came to us during a State visit to Ireland in May 1985. Security was an issue, so the Gardaí arrived with sniffer dogs to check out the Saloon. We had solved the question of who should sit down by removing all but two chairs reserved for our distinguished visitors. We were told that the Crown Prince should be received by me with Gerry to stand one metre behind me. In fact he proved informal and friendly, somewhat to the concern of his earnest palace officials. He bounced into our hall, saying, 'Good morning, good morning'. We greeted him formally in the Saloon. Brendan Kennelly read poetry in English and Irish — the Princess had received some of her education from Irish nuns. We had organised that the mediaeval Brian Boru Harp be moved from the College Library to the House. As the Princess, beautifully dressed and charming in manner entered our library a recording of Carolan music was played. It had been recorded years before when the Harp was conserved in the British Museum. We have not risked playing it since for fear of damage to possibly fragile wood. For the Crown Prince, knowing his interest in fish biology, we had borrowed beautiful illustrations of fish drawn for the first Ordinance Survey of Derry and, I believe, never published. The drawings are kept in the Natural History Museum where I had once been shown them. The Crown Prince spoke of his childhood during World War II, when Ireland seemed to be the only country not at war with Japan. During his journey around Ireland he had been given a box of shamrock by a child. I was to tell him what it was and could it be grown in the imperial garden in Tokyo. I told him I thought so, but that it might be more successful than he would wish.

As the couple left the Provost's House a crowd cheered and waved Japanese flags handed out by a quick thinking official of Foreign

Affairs. The traffic was temporarily reversed to allow the royal couple to proceed down Grafton Street. It had been a big success. The couple returned to Trinity in 2005, now as Emperor Akihito and Empress Michiko, to see the Book of Kells. It was a very welcome second visit.

Subsequently we had several occasions to host Japanese businessmen and scientists and I was well received on a visit to Tokyo. We learned about social relationships with the Japanese — that it was first of all always necessary to exchange personal business cards. Secondly, gifts were beautifully prepared and packaged. Gifts and courtesies on our part were highly valued. There is also a very strong sense of style and high standards in dress. Much deference is given to the senior person present. The ultimate was a dinner in the House when no comments from any of the three junior Japanese present or from some not very verbose Trinity colleagues resulted in the conversation being passed back to the senior on each side who was expected to make the running.

The visit of the Israeli President, Chaim Herzog, in 1985 was also a special occasion. His father had been Chief Rabbi in Dublin and had moved with his family to Palestine, in the years before war broke out in Europe in 1939. Chaim Herzog himself was at school in Dublin at Wesley College and, as he told us, would probably have come to Trinity as a student had his family not emigrated. Gerry, who had lived in Wesley as a junior assistant mistress while she studied in Trinity, sat talking to him on the window-seat of our drawing-room exchanging reminiscences about the Wesley staff. His Dublin visit as a whole was a considerable success because he was able to re-visit the friendships and neighbourhoods of his childhood. We again used the College Library as a resource, showing him maps of Jerusalem from early printed books and a Talmudic scroll. His personal security guards did not speak English, recent immigrants from North Africa to Israel, I think, who conversed with each other in Hebrew.

Visits such as Chaim Herzog's were a potential minefield for disasters of protocol or security but we were fortunate in escaping any serious difficulty throughout our ten years. The appearance of

US Presidents was particularly likely to cause problems. President Reagan did not plan to visit Trinity but the concern for his security was such that we were asked to allow armed US special agents to be located on the roof of the House while his motorcade passed. I refused, stating my willingness to have Gardaí there if necessary — they were to be seen later on the roof above the College's Front Gate. I was conscious of my own sons who had keys to the House gates and who might be endangered by over-zealous security. The Reagan motorcade, with two cars with blacked-out windows so that the President could not be seen, passed on its way to the Dáil with a line of Gardaí standing at close intervals and almost no members of the public on the streets. As a public relations exercise it could hardly have been less successful. An American friend told me that such precautions were unavoidable if US presidents are to make visits, but I question their value except for private consultations if such restrictions must be imposed.

On another occasion in the summer of 1983, when Vice-President H. W. Bush, the father of George W., was visiting the Dáil, his wife Barbara visited the House and was entertained by Gerry. She was very pleasant and outgoing, conversation flowed easily as she walked in our garden on a pleasant sunny day. The disconcerting part was her woman security officer who turned out to be armed with a hand-gun and insisted on first handling any book or photograph that was shown to Mrs Bush.

President Leopold Senghor of Senegal, a distinguished poet in French, visited us in 1983 with the enthusiastic support of our Professor of French, Roger Little, who had lived in West Africa and specialised in the francophone literature of that region. President Senghor read his poetry to a group of academics and students in our Saloon. He was a man of great presence and dignity.

Giscard d'Estaing, temporarily out of politics, but about to plunge in again, was a guest of the then Taoiseach, Garret Fitzgerald. They came to lunch one day. He was a very pleasant lunch companion. I took him to visit the College Library where he was recognised by a large group of visitors who greeted him. Belgians, unfortunately, he said, for he was a man on the election trail.

I visited groups of graduates in many centres in Ireland and Britain with wider travel to Canada, the USA, Australia, Malaysia, Singapore, Hong Kong and Tokyo. I accompanied the Book of Kells to Berlin and Copenhagen. At the end of its travels, I recommended that, for reasons of conservation and security, the Book of Kells should not travel again, if it could be avoided.

Outside the Walls

13.
THE ROYAL IRISH ACADEMY

I WAS ELECTED A MEMBER of the Royal Irish Academy in 1964 and became President for the usual three-year term in 1982, with the encouragement and support of the outgoing president, Proinsias Mac Cana, a distinguished scholar of the Irish Language and Senior Professor at the Dublin Institute for Advanced Studies. When I was a young lecturer the Proceedings of the Academy was a very valuable vehicle for the publication of my research papers. Several detailed studies of interglacial floras in counties Waterford and Limerick appeared there. I was greatly honoured when the Academy was patron of a symposium in honour of my 70th birthday, which resulted in the publication of a *Festschrift* of articles by colleagues with whom I had been closely associated in Ireland and the US and by former graduate students.

One might question whether I was wise to accept the Presidency while Provost of Trinity. I can only say that it worked, but was demanding. When I retired I persuaded Kenneth Whitaker to allow his name to go forward for the Presidency. He had been a very successful civil servant as Secretary of the Department of Finance with much responsibility for moves to modernise the Irish economy during his period in office. At various times he had been Chairman of the Dublin Institute for Advanced Studies, Chancellor of the National University, and an author with a variety of cultural interests, so that his appointment to a purely academic institution was altogether appropriate. The Academy was about to celebrate its 200th anniversary (in 1985) and I wanted to see as President a man who would preside over the year's events, who had a high public profile and was very well respected. The proposal that he should be President was very well received by the Academy.

I spent some of my energies in the previous year trying to raise the Academy's income by fund-raising and increasing membership fees. In practice the Academy's success has involved a slow but steady accretion of new programmes with modest funding. From a slightly dusty old-fashioned place when I was first a member, it has become modernised in well-decorated premises and its facilities and research programmes make steady progress. It is one of the institutions funded by the Higher Education Authority and one of my duties was the annual presentation of our budget, accompanied by Aidan Duggan, the Academy's secretary. Aidan's successful management of our finances contributed significantly to our development.

The Academy is non-political, and this has had the satisfying reward that it is seen as an all-Ireland institution with good representation from Northern Ireland. It gains in academic significance with time and membership is a keenly sought honour.

As President of the Academy I rejoiced in the fact that we are an academic body with academic values and scholarly work as our main purpose. The universities and even the Academy itself are now viewed by the state as important contributors to the 'knowledge economy' and as we seek funding we must have this at the back of our minds. Very great scholars have been members of the Academy in the past and are celebrated in the Academy's bicentennial history (see Bibliography). Sir William Rowan Hamilton was President from 1837 to 1846. The remarkable Edward Hincks is generally agreed to have been a major contributor to the correct reading of Egyptian hieroglyphs and Middle Eastern cuneiform writing, while carrying out his duties as a Church of Ireland clergyman in County Down.

E. G. Quin was one of a long succession of major scholars in Old

Irish. His 'Contributions to the letter S' in the College's annual list of staff publications was an intriguing title, which was part of the Academy's great study for the Dictionary of the Irish Language (DIL). He wrote that 'in spite of its faults DIL constitutes a valuable thesaurus for the early history of Irish'. The Library of the Academy, in itself a very valuable source for scholarly work, houses several manuscripts of great importance to scholarship in Irish. The Academy's major focus on the Irish language, Modern and Old, is now shared with the Dublin Institute for Advanced Studies and the universities. The Proceedings of the Academy have been an important outlet for the publication of reports of major archaeological excavations. Robert Lloyd Praeger contributed greatly to our knowledge of the Irish flora and to a painstaking recording of it county by county. His work is fundamental to conservation of our flora and fauna today. He was responsible for the Academy's invitation to Knud Jessen to whose work Frank Mitchell and I are heavily indebted. There are many other great names amongst its membership.

The modern Academy, structurally divided between Science and the Arts (Polite Literature and Antiquities), is characterised by an ever increasing diversification of its activities and by its role in bringing issues of intellectual interest to a wider public by lectures, seminars, and publications.

The Presidency created opportunities for meeting eminent people at home or abroad. On one occasion I visited the Vatican in my capacity as President at the invitation of the Pontifical Academy of Sciences, a group which advised the Vatican on matters of scientific policy. Its membership included non-Catholic scientists so that His Holiness could hear a wider range of views than he would necessarily hear from a purely Catholic body which would be mindful of and respectful to his known views. On this occasion presidents and representatives of national academies throughout Europe were assembled with representatives from the USA and USSR to discuss the threat of atomic warfare.

We were splendidly housed for two days of deliberation in a beautiful small Renaissance palace in the Vatican Gardens during which we were addressed by Pope John Paul II himself. It was interesting to observe how the meeting was orchestrated. Small countries such as Ireland who had no atomic capability, or desire to have it, said very little. The objective was to commit the representatives of the United States and the Soviet Union to statements about the dangers of atomic warfare and the proliferation of atomic weapons. This was done in what I thought was a skilful and reasonable manner. I was interested to see that the French and British representatives spoke at length but did not seem to realise that they were not equals, except in a debating society manner with the USA and the Soviet Union, whose opinions were the only ones that counted in the long run.

What was the purpose of the meeting? Practically, I think, it helped the Vatican to develop its own concepts for effective policies for peace. I was introduced to Pope John Paul II on two occasions, once in Rome and once in Castel Gandolfo as one of the long line of persons being received. His greetings, heavily accented, were 'Bless you, Ireland' and 'Thank you, Ireland'. When I left I asked if I might view the Sistine Chapel and did so in the empty Chapel with a couple of other Academy Presidents guided by Swiss halberdiers. It was a memorable privilege.

In retrospect I was an odd representative of a largely Catholic nation, but I and others were there as national academy representatives, irrespective of religious belief or lack of it. On my return I reported on the conference to the Academy but was somewhat disappointed that it did not seem to arouse a great deal of interest.

During my Presidency we had a Fine Gael government. Garret Fitzgerald wished to invite Henry Kissinger, who was not then in office, to speak in Ireland. Jim Dooge as Minister for Foreign Affairs approached the Academy to act as host for a lunch which would be held in Iveagh House, the State paying the costs. We agreed with curiosity and some mild apprehension. Kissinger was accompanied by his wife and his son. When the time came to be at Iveagh House, Gerry and I stood at the head of the staircase to receive our guests which included the Taoiseach and much of the government and opposition as well as other distinguished people. It was a strange inversion of the normal order. At lunch and in private conversation Henry Kissinger was an entertaining and courteous companion. Subsequently he addressed his audience on foreign policy in a very forceful cold war mode. The contrast was remarkable, his private persona being much more attractive than his public one. Some of my Academy colleagues thought him an inappropriate guest and were very critical of our role as hosts. Fortunately, they expressed their views so stridently that I benefited from a sympathetic reaction. The controversy died down quickly.

14.
HOSPITALS

MERCER'S HOSPITAL

I FIRST BECAME INVOLVED in hospitals through the agency of W. J. E. (Jerry) Jessop, Professor of Social Medicine, Dean of Medicine and a member of Seanad Éireann. Jerry was very loyal to the Medical School which was in a rather weak position at the time because of competition with Dublin's two other medical schools and the possibility that the State would attempt to close one. Another and more imminent factor was the Fitzgerald Report which proposed closures and amalgamations of small hospitals so that Dublin would finish up with three northside and three southside hospitals. Trinity carried out its teaching through seven small voluntary hospitals whose future was therefore uncertain. All were south of the Liffey.

Jerry was gifted with considerable political skill in forwarding his own plans within and outside College. As he droned on at Board and Council his battered auditors would have given him almost anything to persuade him to stop. His fault, if any, was to ask for too little money even in those impoverished days. He promoted the idea that Trinity should take an interest in the future of the then St Kevin's Hospital, (the future St James's), a large public authority hospital on a big site which had cared for the poorest of patients and the long-stay elderly. It seemed a suitable choice for a large development with the disadvantage that it was derided as 'the poorhouse' by more up-market consultants who didn't want anything to do with it.

As the St James's concept gained in strength and in support from the Department of Health it was proposed to appoint its first board. Provision was made to appoint Board members to represent the seven small voluntary hospitals. He asked me if I would serve as a member of the Mercer's Hospital Board, having ascertained that the Board was willing to appoint me. From this position I could be nominated to the new St James's Board, as indeed came to pass although not with the timing or in the manner which Jerry planned. His intention seemed to be that I would be a 'yes-man' for his plans, a role for which I am temperamentally unsuited, good though those plans were. The outcome was rather funny. After a few rather inconclusive meetings, a new Board of St James's was appointed by the Minister for Health. I was not included, so I was left stranded, so to speak, on the Mercer's Hospital Board with little real knowledge of its business or procedures. I felt in honour bound to do my best for Mercer's and I have never regretted it.

Mercer's was the smallest of the seven voluntary hospitals with 129 beds. It had a small intensive care unit of which it was proud, but it had no distinctive medical speciality, so it was an obvious candidate for early closure. It was a 'Protestant' hospital in the sense that its founder, Mary Mercer, a member of the Church of Ireland about whom relatively little is recorded, provided the funds with which the hospital began its history in 1734. By the 1970s, as with several such small hospitals its Board membership was largely Protestant and its staff at all levels and its patients almost entirely Catholic. In fact this historic survival gave rise to no problems at all and personal relationships were warm and friendly. At first I attended Board meetings, got to know my fellow members and took part in some routine duties.

I enjoyed interviewing candidates to be nurses, together with Matron Mary Kelly. The hospital had an excellent Secretary/Manager in Mr J. P. Little, who controlled expenditure carefully so that our budget always balanced. I calculated that with reasonable care it should easily be possible to set aside 1% of our budget of about £2 million to improve equipment. This was done and it resulted in some improvement in the replacement of out-of-date gear. Finally I became Chairman, I don't remember the circumstances, but some of the older Board members had retired or died and I think there was a realisation of the necessity for closure, but a reluctance to do it. I was an obvious candidate because of my links to Trinity as Provost and to St James's and the wider world of medical politics.

In 1982 the question of closure became pressing, dates were mentioned, but the Department of Health seemed to find it difficult to make a decision, and there was a depressing sense of aimless drift. I persuaded my colleagues that it was better to decide on a closure date ourselves and to close with dignity and a clear view of the future rather than be forced into an ignominious closure one or two years later. I met with a group of consultants and they agreed, understandably with some reservation and uncertainty.

One important consideration was that, if we were the first hospital to close we could expect to save the jobs of our staff by transfer to St James's. The job horizons for younger staff at all levels were potentially attractive. In the outcome it all worked. All the jobs were transferred to St James's for those who wished to go. The great majority of the staff and the consultants either moved fully to St James's or had contracts with other hospitals also. One younger consultant, Peter Daly, who by Department rules could only be a general physician at Mercer's, was at last allowed to develop his special skill in oncology at St James's. We owe a considerable debt to Pat Corcoran, Personnel Officer, Federated Dublin Voluntary Hospitals, Desmond Dempsey, his Chief Executive and Liam Dunbar, Chief Executive at St James's who, between them, demonstrated that it was possible to close hospitals in a reasonable and sensitive way without excessive delay. The hospital closed in May 1983 in a very emotional farewell party, the stress level raised greatly by the death of one of our consultants, Dick Brenan, in the hospital a few hours before closure on the last day.

When the hospital closed there were some surprises. One of the older nurses turned out to have no close relatives and nowhere to live other than the hospital. We bought her a small house in the north of the city. By present day standards she did enormously well but there was a good deal of pragmatism attached to obtaining a closure with minimum hurt and resentment.

Finally the hospital was sold to the College of Surgeons for £850,000. It has become the centre of the College's Library, houses student residences and is the location of an effective general practice. We decided to use the funds available for the support of the sick poor of Dublin in accordance with Mary Mercer's intentions and we established a Foundation for that purpose. The Department of Health believed that it should inherit the Hospital's funds but we maintained that the funds were the property of the Board, provided they were applied to the founder's original intentions. The Department had indeed funded the hospital for most of its activities in recent years but I used the, perhaps rather frivolous, analogy of a motorist who buys his petrol from the same garage for many years but does not expect to own the garage. So, the Mercer's Hospital Foundation came into being to manage funds resulting from the sale of the Hospital building. The Foundation's Board, with up to ten members, was established according to a cy-près scheme approved by the Courts.

Over a period of years the invested value of the fund has risen to over €7 million. The Trustees meet twice annually to disburse money. We limit our support to the provision of medical services rather than research or the creation of permanent posts. We have supported general practice in the Royal College of Surgeons, and geriatric services in St James's Hospital through Davis Coakley, Professor of Medical Gerontology at Trinity College, and his colleagues.

The Department of Public Health and Primary Care in Trinity College, under the vigorous leadership of Tom O'Dowd, Professor of General Practice, has developed general practice in the Jobstown (West Tallaght) area of the city, a deprived area of public housing with significant social problems. In collaboration with the Eastern Health Board we made funding available for the building of the Mary Mercer Health Centre at Jobstown. Incredibly, the £1.5 million we had available was not taken up because of legal delays and other problems. An enormous amount of effort went into the unimaginable task of persuading a Health Authority to accept a large gift, not helped, as we were, by the creation of new authorities (Eastern Health Board to South-Western Area Health Board, to something else at the end of 2004) each of which had its own legal advisers, was slow to engage in any partnership with a private organisation which might reduce its authority, and did not seem able to recognise how much could be done with an unplanned windfall. Technically, the centre has been a resounding success and will provide a model of the sort of health centre that will take some pressure off acute hospitals and supply many local needs. We continue to support general practice at Tallaght by funding an appointment, but, finally in frustration, withdrew the offer of capital funding.

TALLAGHT

At Mercer's we were the first to close a hospital, at a time when it seemed that the Department of Health was too afraid of opposition to implement its own policies. My involvement with Mercer's together with a fatal inability to say 'no' then led to a whole range of hospital activities. I became Chairman of the Central Council of the Federated Dublin Voluntary Hospitals, a body bringing together the seven hospitals due for closure, which still had administrative functions. The Council became increasingly irrelevant and time-wasting as the futures of the individual hospitals were determined by bodies external to it. In spite of frequent reminders the Department of Health delayed and delayed in bringing the Council to its statutory end.

In fairness, the task of developing new hospital services to replace the old hospitals was very complex and huge in scale, involving major capital expenditure in site development and construction, with very large resources needed for personnel and equipment. It is a near-miracle that two modern hospitals emerged, the new hospital at Tallaght by 1996, both hospitals continuing to develop new facilities. The history of the emergence of the new model St James's Hospital is set out very clearly by Professor Peter Gatenby in *The Feds*, pages 19–24, a fine study edited by David Fitzpatrick (see Bibliography) and for Tallaght by Desmond Rogan in the same study, pages 53–64. *The Feds* covers many aspects of the history and evolution of the original seven hospitals and may be consulted for detail.

It became all too clear, to a recent arrival on the Council like myself, why progress in hospital closure and amalgamation had been so slow. There were conflicting medical and professional interests, even political interests where the membership of a hospital board included local authority representatives. A pathology laboratory for all the hospitals had been established at St James's, but the Meath/Adelaide/National Children's Hospital (MANCH) group of hospitals believed passionately that their needs were not met fairly. At various times I served on the Boards of the Meath Hospital, of Dr Steevens' Hospital and of Baggot Street Hospital. Sir Patrick Dun's, like Mercer's, went almost entirely to the expanding St James's as did some of the staff from Baggot Street and Dr Steevens'. St James's steadily emerged as a very major hospital fully supported by the Department of Health. What was then to happen to the MANCH axis? The decision was for a new hospital at Tallaght, a rapidly growing suburb, a medium sized town in its own right, in southwest Dublin.

The early development of the Tallaght Hospital (technically now the Adelaide and Meath Hospital, Dublin, incorporating the National Children's Hospital) was rather slow and confusing. A Board was set up in 1981 by the Minister for Health to build the new hospital. It was officially opened three times by different Ministers before any building took place with enormous increases in cost at each successive stage. I attended a meeting in the National Children's Hospital in Harcourt Street to hear the then Minister for Health, Barry Desmond, announce that the building which we thought would cost £60 million would probably cost at least £100 million.

The question arose as to Trinity's role at Tallaght. The three

MANCH hospitals to be united there provided close to 50% of the clinical teaching needs and places for the College's students. As Provost I took the view that the Medical School would continue to need access to teaching in the new hospital to provide the diversity of disciplines that would be required by a large teaching institute. This view was disputed by several senior consultants at St James's who maintained that St James's was large enough for all Trinity's requirements and that Tallaght would cause the College's always insufficient finances to be too thinly spread. I explained to one colleague that I saw the three hospitals, with which the College had been associated over a long period, as part of the College's heritage, and they should not be regarded as easily dispensable. This was a gut-feeling but the argument for the necessity of sufficient access to enough disciplines and beds was then and still is quite clear to me. Some colleagues feared jealousies and competition between St James's and Tallaght such as could occasionally be observed between the Mater and St Vincent's, the two UCD-linked hospitals. There was, and is, some validity in this concern, but not enough to override the need for adequate teaching access. If the argument that Dublin did not need three medical schools and that one should be closed should ever arise again I did not want Trinity to be the one to close. Fortunately closure of any medical school no longer seems likely and the expansion of medical services is constantly required.

In 1989 a meeting took place between representatives of the Tallaght Hospital Board and the College to determine Trinity's future position at Tallaght. The Board was represented by Professor Richard Conroy, the Board's Chairman, Dr Gerry Hurley, Mr Michael Butler and Mr Desmond Rogan, the Board's acting secretary. I represented the College, accompanied by Ian Temperley, then Dean of the Faculty of Health Sciences, and by Salters Sterling, the Academic Secretary who subsequently became a member of the Adelaide and Meath Board.

The College was caught between a rock and a hard place. We wanted our place in Tallaght but didn't easily see how to pay for it. We were pressed by the Tallaght Board representatives to make our intentions clear about the nature of our future relationship, if any, with the proposed hospital. I declared that it was clearly Trinity's intention to be the University associated with the hospital. We would ask the Board of the College to enter into a Teaching Agreement with the Hospital which would replicate the existing Teaching Agreement with St James's and give it the same status with the College as was already enjoyed by St James's. We proposed that a Chair in Medicine and a Chair in Surgery be created at Tallaght and a Clinical Sciences Building be erected for which a minimum of £1 million would be available from the College. The Teaching Agreement was signed in 1995, and the Clinical Sciences Building opened in 2000. Interviews for the Chair of Medicine took place in 2001 and for the Chair of Surgery in 2002. So what had felt uncomfortably like financial brinkmanship in 1989 had been achieved in my successor's time.

The Medical School with its two hospitals is now a very large activity — the budget for the two hospitals greatly exceeds the College's annual budget. There is a very large School of Nursing as part of the College and many other activities in different medical disciplines. It is notable that the election to Dean of Medicine now has a larger electorate than the electorate to the Provostship. Jerry Jessop would have been proud of it.

MEATH HOSPITAL

I joined the Board of Baggot Street (Royal City of Dublin) Hospital for a short period but concluded that I really had very little to contribute and resigned. My links with the Meath Hospital were more substantial. I was proposed for election to its Board by a group of consultants and served for one period, not then seeking re-election. Closure was on the horizon and the Board had given very little thought to the future. I suggested to the members that as they were, as far as I could judge, the owners of the Hospital collectively as Board members, it would be timely to consider what to do with the funding that would be released when the Hospital was sold. This idea seems to have borne fruit because there is now a Meath

Hospital Foundation which funds activities at the new Tallaght Hospital. Such Foundations in several of the closed hospitals keep up a valuable tradition of independent voluntary service which can parallel several of the activities of the Department of Health without being swallowed up by it.

DR STEEVENS' HOSPITAL

My membership of the Board of Dr Steevens' Hospital was short-lived though very active. I do not recollect the circumstances in which I was invited to serve, but probably it arose because of my experience of the Mercer's closure given that the closure of Dr Steevens' was also planned. Most of my activity within the Hospital was of a routine nature with uncertainty about the future prominent in the Board's discussions. The subject was divisive with several strong currents of disagreement about what was best to do with its 210 beds. Dr Steevens' was one of the largest of the seven hospitals in which Trinity carried out its teaching. Its budget two years before closure was about £4 million.

The future plan on which the Board relied was that the Hospital would cease to provide services in general medicine and surgery and also in specialties in plastic surgery, maxillo-facial surgery and accident and emergency services which would, in the main, be re-located at St James's Hospital. Some Accident and Emergency beds might be provided in the Meath Hospital. The assumption was that Dr Steevens' would remain open as a centre for orthopaedics until the new Hospital at Tallaght came on stream in about 2006 (twenty years ahead!). In the year prior to closure (1987) the Hospital's budget was halved to about £2 million and it was apparent that the Hospital was close to, if not actually at, insolvency, given the size of the cut. The financial crisis made the Hospital totally dependent on the Department of Health and made any possibility of continuing as a specialist orthopaedic hospital unlikely.

On May 28 1987 the Chairman of the Board, Mr B. G. Campbell, and the Secretary/Manager, Mr D. S. Hope, reported that they had been summoned urgently at noon on the previous day to meet with officials of the Department of Health, Comhairle an nOspidéal, and, surprisingly, the Eastern Health Board. The officials explained that the state of the national finances dictated that its rationalisation plan be implemented as soon as possible and that Dr Steevens' Hospital would have to close within three to four months.

The Hospital issued a press release shortly afterwards in response to newspaper reports on its closure. It stated that 'it was distressing to read a statement in the newspapers purporting to come from the Department of Health implying that essential services would have to be moved to other Hospitals as a result of Dr Steevens' Board's unilateral decision'. Exactly what the unilateral decision was is unclear. There may have been a complete misunderstanding of the Hospital's plans for orthopaedic services. Elsewhere the press release records that the officials asked if the agreement of Dr Steevens' Board could be obtained quickly. The Hospital's representatives enquired if it would make any difference whether agreement was obtained or not. The reply was that rationalisation would go ahead anyway.

There was certainly a great deal of anger and stress at the time of closure, more than was true of any other of the seven Federated Hospitals. It is possible to look at the effect of the decision with some detachment today nearly twenty years later. The loss of some 210 beds, some of which had been assigned to Accident and Emergency, was a serious matter. Some of the beds were replaced by subsequent expansion at St James's. One of the most serious losses was the possibility to have an effective Orthopaedic Centre. The orthopaedic surgeons were not provided with adequate bed replacements and the situation persisted that skilled surgeons anxious to exercise their professional skills had inadequate access to beds and operating theatres in the Adelaide Hospital which itself was overstretched already. Hip replacement operations for which waiting lists were already a problem, were reduced in number. Finally, the Department having itself caused the Hospital insoluble financial problems by the savagery of its budget cuts, used the

Hospital's budgetary position to force it to close and to accept a punitive settlement.

I hope now that the Department officials who were responsible for the decisions would reflect on them and ask themselves 'Why did we do this, why were we so angry?' If the decision was for closure (the Hospital had accepted that it was) could it not have been done in some more decent way that recognised the Hospital's long history of public service, which was being valued at nothing. At this distance one can understand that the Department was at the time under extreme pressure for budget cuts. It is, however, not necessary to believe that the right decisions were taken. Bed closures then were the harbingers of patients on trolleys in the corridors of Accident and Emergency departments today.

THE WORTH LIBRARY

The Dr Steevens' Board met in the Worth Library. The Library was a collection of books mainly from the period of construction of the Hospital with limited later additions. The collection had two outstanding qualities, the first that it represented a record of the intellectual life and interests of Edward Worth, an eighteenth century professional man and bibliophile. In particular there were some interesting early medical texts. Secondly it had some exceptionally beautiful fine bindings. These are described in an Irish Arts Review issue (see Bibliography) by Muriel McCarthy, the Librarian of Marsh's Library who also advised the Worth Library. The books and bindings are undoubtedly very valuable and could raise great interest if sold but there never was an intention on anybody's part to sell any part of the collection. The room also contained portraits of Dr Richard Steevens and of his sister Griselda (Grizel) who secured the site where the hospital was built. Much interesting information on the hospital and on Dr Worth's Library can be found in *The Feds* (see Bibliography). It was a room full of character and atmosphere. The Library was well-known to a limited circle of people with interests in history and architecture but was little visited and not used as a working library unless for research purposes.

The question arose, what would happen to the library on closure. The Eastern Health Board was already a potential future owner of the Hospital building, but the Board members had not imagined that a Health Board would want the building for anything but offices and had not thought of the Library's future. I suggested that the Library and its pictures should be transferred to the Trinity Library pending any necessary further action. I believed that the Library should be permanently re-located in Trinity.

When the Hospital was closed it emerged that the Eastern Health Board (EHB) had elaborate plans to refurbish the building and pressed the case that the Worth Library should be returned to it. Agreement could not be reached and finally the EHB decided to take Trinity to court on the issue. The case was heard in the Four Courts with Mr Justice Keane presiding. The long judgment, which I think would require a well-informed Senior Counsel to understand, essentially gave the victory to the EHB so the books and the art-work were returned. My understanding of the essence of the judgment was that the books were part of the hospital and must remain there. At least this would protect the Library from a future commercial sale. I attended the court case daily. I had retired as Provost and had continued to take an interest in the case by agreement with my successor. I was greatly disappointed at the outcome.

Several aspects of the Worth Library case occur to me. The EHB clearly wanted a prestigious new headquarters and may well have required better office space, but was a historic library part of their needs? The presence of EHB representation at the meeting of Steevens' Board members with the Department of Health on closure suggests an already close interest in the future of the Hospital buildings. But was the Library and the High Court case a proper way to spend public money that should be dedicated to provision of health care? The EHB had no professional staff with expertise in historical libraries. It finally arranged with Trinity Library to maintain an oversight on the collection, ultimately setting up a local management committee. When the EHB purchased the Hospital the Board had not considered that the Library was included in the price. Effectively, as a result of Mr Justice Keane's judgment the EHB gained the Library at no cost.

One of the worst features of the legal judgment was that the opinions of the Board of Dr Steevens' Hospital were treated, literally, as of no significance whatsoever. Thus a Board which for many years had managed the Hospital and its finances in a voluntary capacity now found its decision suddenly overturned. It could dispose of beds and medical equipment and discuss the future of staff but could not make decisions about the Worth Library. It was ironic that as the Dr Steevens' Hospital Board passed into history after nearly three centuries, the EHB in one of the many protean transformations of the Health Services has already disappeared into something else, becoming part of the newly established Health Service Executive.

HEALTH RESEARCH BOARD

Barry Desmond, TD, then Minister for Health, invited me to become Chairman of a new body, the Health Research Board (HRB), which would shortly begin its work. We met in his office at the Custom House for a briefing on the issues involved. The first meeting of the Board, which he addressed, took place on the 7th January 1987. The new Board would amalgamate the functions of the pre-existing Medical Research Council and the Medico-Social Research Board. My task was to try to bring the two bodies into reasonable harmony with one another, showing no partiality, in the knowledge that neither was initially particularly happy about a common future. It did, however, work out quite well, both sides showing a good degree of courtesy and tolerance to one another and not seeking confrontation. There were obvious anxieties about the distribution of funding and the respect that would be shown to the disciplines involved, but, in retrospect, the union has really

171

worked and not left difficulties behind. The success owes much to the excellent administrative staff involved.

At the beginning, funding was a major problem that would lead to my resignation as Chairman three years later. A total expenditure of £3 million in 1987 fell to £2.4 million in each of 1989, 1990 and 1991 by which time I had resigned. By the mid-90s the budget had climbed to £5 million, subsequently increasing by important increments annually to €20.2 million in 2002 and €27.4 million in 2003. This very much better figure is still low by comparison with the more developed European Union countries.

Vivian O'Gorman, newly appointed Chief Executive of the HRB, wrote to the Minister for Health (Rory O'Hanlon) on the 15th November 1989 to protest that the £1.3 million provided in the Book of Estimates for 1990 was the same as had been provided in 1989 and did not even provide for inflation. These figures were a severe cut from £2.3 million in 1988. Vivian had already had the very dispiriting experience of seeing his budget cut heavily on the day he was appointed. I was very pleased that we had recruited him because I knew the quality of his performance as an administrator in the National Board for Science and Technology (NBST). To quote Vivian in writing to the Minister, 'It means that in relation to the Board's core activities, i.e. research grants, epidemiological research, research units, summer student grants and science degree scholarships, no new starts can be funded in 1990. Effectively ... our national medical and health research programme was no longer viable'!

Rory O'Hanlon replied by a letter signed by his private secretary of which I cite excerpts. 'The Government must take account of the competing demands for Exchequer funding and must allocate scarce resources in accordance with the priority of needs. In the current economic context the Minister considers that the provision made for the Board is a reasonable one'. In further observations the Minister drew our attention to savings he believed we could make by more rigorous examination of our expenditures, his hopes for EU funding, and his belief that we were 'in a strong position to generate non-Exchequer funding for valuable research programmes'.

In brief the Minister for Health would not, or could not, defend health research which should not have been omitted from his Department's priorities and which I had a duty to defend. I had already expressed my extreme disappointment at the 1989 Book of Estimates and had indicated that I would live with it for a year under protest provided the funding level of previous years was restored in 1990. If it were not, I would resign. I obtained an interview with Minister O'Hanlon and told him of the impossible position his lack of action created for my Board and for myself. He was quite unmoved, and said very little. Later in the same day, 22nd November 1989, the Board met in emergency session at which I resigned saying that I could not continue. I walked out. Professor Muiris Fitzgerald of UCD succeeded me as Chairman.

I had no regrets about my departure, then or since. I was very angry with Rory O'Hanlon and his senior officials. Senior officials are supposed to guide their Minister away from making silly mistakes. None of them was prepared to stand up to what I assume was pressure from the Department of Finance at a time of perceived financial crisis. They should have had a better sense of the core values of their Department from which research could not be omitted. I had left my excellent colleagues on the Board to pick up the bits, but, if my resignation did any good, it may have shaken the torpor and complacency of the Department into setting matters right in later years. I was delighted when the Board decided some years later to award a Watts Medal annually for the best performing student in summer research projects. The medal probably has more to do with my historical role as first Chairman than with my ill-starred jousting with Rory O'Hanlon, but in any case it gave much pleasure to me.

15.
CONSERVATION

AN TAISCE

ALTHOUGH MY MAIN conservation interest has been in natural habitats and wildlife, I became very involved for some years in architecture and the urban environment. This arose from my membership of An Taisce, the National Trust for Ireland, in the 1960s. The organisation had been founded in the years after the war in a spirit of enthusiasm but this had faded and there was a low level of activity with an out-of-date list of members and a weak financial base. I was elected Secretary by the council of An Taisce (1966–67) and later, for two years, Chairman (1967–69). George Bagnall of Bord Fáilte and I invited Kevin Fox, a lecturer in planning at Bolton Street and with considerable standing among architects, and Joseph McCullough, a structural engineer very well informed on urban issues, to join us in an effort to put An Taisce on the map. The result was the publication of the Amenity Study of Dublin and Dun Laoghaire (1967) which was associated with an exhibition of photographs of buildings recommended for protection. Kevin Fox was the major author of the study. The exhibition and the publication drew a considerable public response and greatly increased membership to about 800 from a low base. An Taisce had been given official status under the Local Government Planning and Development Act of 1963. It was now entitled to receive copies of planning applications and to comment on them to the local authority involved. This became a major pre-occupation of the Trust, for the sheer volume of paper generated nationwide was beyond our capacity to handle without a professional staff yet the interest of the Trust was deeply involved in the quality of applications for development and for modification or demolition of existing buildings.

The possibility that An Taisce would become a major owner of heritage sites as originally envisaged was unrealistic because of its very modest finances. Its emphasis became protection of the architectural and natural environments by using the planning process. Its role came to be a voice against the most rapacious developers and a vehicle for development of public opinion. Frank McDonald, an Irish Times journalist, writing on planning and development issues in his *The Destruction of Dublin* thought that An Taisce 'has always been a fairly timid organisation'. This may be true for those who prefer public confrontation but it seems to me that the establishment of a large body of moderate opinion in the middle ground, that cannot be dismissed as a small bunch of cranks or extremists, has its own merit.

I ceased to be Chairman of An Taisce after two years in office. There were others now keen to play a role and it was time to stand down. David Jeffrey of Trinity's Botany Department joined the Council of An Taisce with my encouragement and subsequently played a major role as President (1997–2002) in helping the organisation develop its shape and focus.

NATIONAL PARKS

I have always been interested in wildlife and the countryside. By the mid-1960s, I had become very concerned about the damage to our landscape caused by all sorts of intrusive development. There is focus now on inappropriate housing development but I was more responsive to the impact of forestry, peat-cutting and drainage on natural vegetation.

I particularly recall one occasion. During the war years the Military Road from the Sally Gap to Laragh in County Wicklow had not been maintained. When I was sixteen or seventeen I rode my bike along what had become a really terrible road; at the worst sections I had to carry my bike. It was a lovely early summer day with blue skies and scattered fleecy cloud. Looking back towards Djouce I saw a virgin mountainside, quite untouched in shades of brown and yellow and utterly remote and beautiful. I have never forgotten that vision. About twenty years ago I drove along the same road on a hot summer day. There were conifer plantations over large areas and scars caused by service roads and drains. There were several heather fires that day caused by discarded cigarettes and picnickers, the landscape disfigured by burnt patches. I hardly ever follow that road now and am always oppressed by the sight of such wrecked landscapes.

I formed the view that much had been irreparably damaged in Ireland and that the protection of the remaining natural landscapes should be a priority. I made a start at Killarney. As secretary of An Taisce and, in that capacity with John Jackson, a member, and Director of the Natural History Museum, I sought an interview with Donogh O'Malley, then the Junior Minister in Finance, with responsibility for the Office of Public Works. The Killarney National Park, the only one in the country at that time, was under threat from uncontrolled grazing by sheep introduced by An Foras Talúntais with the approval of the OPW. There was also a threat from a proposal that Muckross House be assigned to the Institute of Public Administration as a conference centre. I made the case, to the Minister and to Commissioner Cullinane of the OPW, that the legislation regulating the Park made it clear that Muckross House could not be so assigned and that grazing should be eliminated in the most sensitive areas of the Park. Donogh O'Malley listened and acknowledged that I had made a good case and that he would look into it. Months later we called on him again to point to lack of progress. Commissioner Cullinane was again present and said that he thought we would have got tired and gone away. However the Minister and the OPW did move. The threat to Muckross House went away as did the sheep. I owe it to Donogh O'Malley to record that the first positive steps were taken during his Ministry.

Shortly afterwards a new Commissioner, later to be Chairman, arrived in the person of John McCarthy. John had had little contact with conservation before he arrived from an earlier position managing OPW's supplies and stores (he just counted nuts and bolts his critics said). He quickly immersed himself in conservation projects and became very well informed. He was a top class civil servant and a good friend. I became convinced that a conservation lobby dedicated to criticising the public service was going nowhere. He adopted policies which favoured the expansion of the national parks system.

I believed that it was necessary to consolidate the Killarney National Park by purchasing the remaining substantial estates in private ownership in the Killarney Valley and, ideally, to control the water-courses feeding the Killarney Lakes to limit pollution. Over the next few years much of this happened and there was no further encroachment of conifer plantations. Killarney Town acquired a new treatment plant for sewage and waste water and Muckross House, managed by Trustees, became a visitor centre for ever-increasing tourist numbers.

Practical estate management took the form of fenced exclosures which quickly proved the impact of grazing on woodland regeneration and which led to a programme of culling sika deer, an exotic species introduced or escaped from private estates which was all too abundant. *Rhododendron ponticum*, an invasive non-native competitor within the natural oak woods, was cut from large areas. The Park near Muckross House had old estate walks. I designed and wrote texts for three walks of varying length through the woods, which were designed to tempt exploration beyond visitor centres. There is still much work to be done to manage the National Park. Once, when I was impatient at slow progress, John said to me, 'You've got to remember, Bill, the Civil Service goes on for ever.'

We used to meet at the County Club in Churchtown in the Christmas season to discuss plans. We were usually joined by Pascal Scanlan, who subsequently became Chairman of the Commissioners, and George Bagnall of Bord Fáilte, an engineer with great sensitivity to the environment and promoter of the inland waterways system under Tim O'Driscoll's friendly chairmanship of Bord Fáilte. Others included Sidney Maskell who was concerned with OPW gardens. On one such occasion John asked me where there should be national parks in Ireland. I drew a map of Ireland on a paper napkin identifying the Burren, Connemara, Donegal, Wicklow (perhaps) and somewhere in the Shannon Valley with waterways and peatlands. There is a rumour that the napkin still exists on file in the OPW! I argued that, at this time, we should try to establish parks in areas of outstanding importance because of their wildlife and flora where large tracts were in single ownership (because of the legal complexities of common ownership of grazing land). Compared with Britain, land in Ireland was then relatively cheap and much of its wild areas thinly inhabited or uninhabited. Other considerations would, of course, prevail today.

After Killarney I had become acquainted with Henry McIlhenny, owner of the Glenveagh Estate in north County Donegal. The estate had some good oak and yew woodland and a red deer population, descended from a Scottish importation. The yews are the most northerly population in the British Isles, for there does not seem to be any of certain natural status in Scotland. Mr McIlhenny entertained many guests for deer hunting expeditions. I recollect Bing Crosby being one of them. Once when I was on the estate an injured deer bleeding on its side ran by. It had been shot, but not fatally, and would, I think, finally die from blood loss and exhaustion unless its hunter caught up and dispatched it. I do not like to see wild animals killed for sport but I recognise that, in the absence of natural predators, some culling is necessary in deer populations, which will otherwise trash their habitat by overgrazing. Once I climbed in October up the steep side of the Glenveagh Valley to the moorland above. The red deer were in their breeding season. The stags strutted and bellowed and charged about. I walked among them, perhaps a dangerous thing to do, but an exhilarating experience.

The OPW were persuaded that Glenveagh was a potential National Park. John McCarthy opened negotiations to purchase and it all came to pass. Henry McIlhenny was an elderly man with no obvious heirs and he was willing to sell provided he retained residence rights in the Castle. A visit to him was a great experience. If you called in mid-morning he was apt to receive you in his four poster canopied bed wearing a heavy ornate dressing gown. On the day the formal transfer took place in pouring rain, Richie Ryan, the then Minister for Finance, represented the State. We lunched on venison with magnificent plate and uniformed servants.

When Glenveagh became a National Park, a centre was established where visitors could obtain information about the Park. The OPW initially feared that the Park would not be a success, because it was too remote. This has not proved to be so. It has had about 100,000 visitors a year and, no doubt, generates much good to the local economy. From my own perspective as a natural scientist, a large bog, a big area of heath and some rare woodland have been preserved. Exclosures in the woodland, as at Killarney, have allowed the regeneration of natural woodland previously hammered by deer grazing and plants have reappeared that had been grazed almost out of existence.

The woods and the Park yield rare birds, woodwarblers and redstarts, and I have had the joy of seeing red-throated divers on the lake, northern birds at their extreme southern limit in north-west Ireland. Golden Eagles which became extinct in Ireland shortly after 1900 have been re-introduced from Scottish stock to the Glenveagh area, a very suitable habitat. A pair has begun nest building. Most of the Park is wild and little visited; visitors tend to stick to the neighbourhood of the Visitor Centre and Castle and not penetrate far into the wilderness. This use pattern is common in National Parks, a small percentage of the area used intensively, the rest quite wild, a happy marriage of tourist and conservation interests. I was startled recently to see, in a BBC programme on Neanderthal Man, what I recognised as moorland overlooking the Glenveagh Valley in winter, apparently to model the sort of hostile climatic environment in which early human types became extinct.

After the successful creation of the Glenveagh Park work began on the Connemara National Park, focussed on Letterfrack and the

Twelve Bens. This is based on an area of bare mountain and bogland. I would have liked, and still would like, to see the inclusion of some of the low-elevation very wet blanket bog and mazy lakes, lying between Roundstone and the area just south of Clifden. There is a major concentration of rare and even very rare native plants in this area, including several heaths. One, *Erica mackaiana*, occurs here locally, but one has to jump to Spain and Portugal for the major part of its range.

Most remarkable is *Erica ciliaris*, the Dorset Heath. It was collected once in the 19th century by Mackay and a good dried specimen exists in Trinity College's Botany Herbarium, but it was generally believed to be a misrecording of a plant collected in southern England, where there is a significant population in one small area. The question was resolved when my colleague David Webb parked his car one day on the back road from Roundstone to Clifden and stepped out into a patch of the uncertain *Erica*. The patch, the size of a suburban drawing room seems to be all that there is, so it is one of our super-rare plants. This area continues to turn up new botanical surprises. The best place to find exciting new plants seems to be where there is already a rich flora.

I will conclude with the Burren. I have always had a deep affection for it and have visited it on many occasions in the last 50 years. I particularly like Mullaghmore, a strangely tortured limestone mountain with one largish lake and some small lakes at its base. There is a wood which contains all of Ireland's woody species except oak and alder which dislike the Burren's limestone, but whitebeam, crabapple, buckthorns and dogwood are there in a wood of ash and hazel, with native elm, now ravaged by Dutch Elm disease. Of course gentians, *Dryas* and uncommon orchids and many other plants are there around the big lake. There are unusual butterflies. I have watched an otter lazily bathing in the lake, sat on the cliff above it to watch a fox picking his way over the pavements and, once, to my delight, while driving, on a backroad towards the lake, telling an English visitor that pine martens could be seen there, turned a corner to find one crossing the road in no great hurry, yielding a splendid view. Moments like this come once in a lifetime but are bright memories for ever.

My Burren enthusiasm was such that I raised money from Trinity Trust, a graduate organisation, with a view to buying the base of Mullaghmore for study and research by the Botany Department. I negotiated with a local farmer and for £1,300 became the possessor of more than 60 acres of prime land including part of the big lake, a small lake, a wood and much limestone pavement and small cliffs. My plan was to use the site for botanical studies and research, especially to assess the significance of grazing in maintaining or damaging the flora. At one extreme, overgrazing by goats and cattle could press very hard on sensitive species. Yews, for example, were reduced to pincushion shape and size, but grew well out of cliff faces where goats yet scrambled out on trunks and branches to eat the foliage. At the other extreme, too luxurious ungrazed growth might overwhelm the small plants that are the joy of the Burren. In either event I was defeated by logistics; it was just too far from Dublin to sustain the research. I approached the OPW with the suggestion that they might purchase our plot as a central part of a new Burren National Park to which other properties could be added by purchase. The sale was completed for £13,000 with the sole condition that the land be used solely to conserve the native flora and fauna. The mark-up seems large but was realistic in relation to the pace of inflation. It seems very small now when one considers the huge amounts of money spent on car parks, potential visitor centres, and such, which came to nothing.

I took no part in the controversies about visitor centres and parking places which raged subsequently in the Burren. The waste of time and money was deplorable with no worthwhile outcome, but it caused me to think out my own position and why trouble arose. A large part of the problem was because of a failure, within our own political culture of clientelism, to recognise what purpose National Parks serve. The primary purpose is to protect and conserve plants and animals which are the real clients. Every Minister responsible should ask what proportion of his budget goes to actual conservation as protection, research or necessary data bases. Now a successful National Park is naturally attractive to tourists and can be given a focus by a visitor centre which can provide information, maps, refreshments and other facilities. If one starts from the view that the Park's purpose is to provide jobs, encourage tourism, and promote clientelism then things go wrong.

I did not take part in the establishment of the Wicklow National Park though I am glad that it has been identified. I took part as Chairman on a committee to advise on the establishment of a National Park in Mayo. Our advice was accepted and a large block of wild peatland and mountain southeast of Bangor Erris towards Nephinbeg was purchased by negotiation with local landowners. The establishment of the Park was approved by Síle de Valera as the responsible Minister and by Mayo County Council. There was a problem about identifying a park centre. The choice was left to the Minister, and there were delays before work commenced on the centre at Ballycroy. The Centre was planned to be complete and open to visitors in 2008, and the Park was to be named Ballycroy National Park. Meanwhile progress is being made with a management plan and a study of the conservation issues. I hope that a reasonable proportion of the available budget will go to the study of the plant and animal life of the Park and to the appointment of scientific staff. It will then be ready to welcome visitors.

Much of my interest has been in peatland, woodland and landscape preservation in general. I was much stimulated by The Hon. Miriam Rothschild, a member of a famous family, several of whom had deep interests in the natural sciences and conservation. Her father had visited Ireland in the early 1900s to draw up a list of peatland areas which he thought should be conserved. She wished to honour her father's initiative by following up his ideas on sites that should be conserved. She came to Ireland several times and lobbied me to pursue peatland conservation. This led to my visiting, in my An Taisce capacity, the offices of the Land Commission which was then closing down its activities. I visited any bogland still in the Commission's ownership and they agreed to transfer a large almost untouched bog at Addergoole in the Suck Valley near Ahascragh, Co. Galway, to An Taisce ownership and on another day, nearly 4000 acres of wild mountain bogland and rock south of Lough Nacung in North Donegal for the traditional shilling. To my anger, Bord na Móna refused to honour an agreement plainly made in good faith that the Ahascragh peatland would not be exploited. Instead Mongan's Bog near Clonmacnoise, a much smaller but valuable site, was offered in exchange and was better than nothing. The Bord na Móna attitude was that they had powers of compulsory purchase, verbal promises meant nothing in face of the commercial possibility of peatland exploitation, and conservation was for the impractical and wimpish, an outlook still all too prevalent.

As part of my activities in nature conservation I worked for a period as a part-time advisor to An Foras Forbartha, an organisation promoting research and study into planning issues. I prepared lists of sites of scientific interest by county indicating areas of concentration of rare species or exceptional habitats. Inevitably the work could not be comprehensive, there was too much to do for one person, but the resulting lists alerted local authorities to areas they should take measures to protect and laid some foundations for the far more detailed studies which followed. The State still has great difficulty in taking its duties in nature conversation as seriously as it should. The constant criticism by the European Commission shows the insufficiency of resources and trained personnel to carry out the essential measures.

16.
FOTA HOUSE AND GARDENS

AFTER MY RETIREMENT IN the Summer of 1991, I received a visit from Tom Raftery, Professor of Agriculture in University College, Cork, accompanied by the late Aidan Brady, Director of the National Botanic Gardens. They asked me to consider becoming Chairman of the recently created Fota Trust which, when fully established, would have responsibility for the conservation of the historic Fota House and Gardens. There was difficulty because of vigorous public controversy, fully reported in the media, about management of the Fota Estate and especially about tree-felling. The whole subject had become a hot potato which few were willing to pick up. Tom and Aidan thought it desirable to find a Chairman who had not been involved in the local controversies and who, in my case, was a botanist with, above all, a track-record in fund-raising.

I asked for time to consider the proposal, but I was quite tempted by something new to do in my retirement, in spite of the apparent maelstrom into which I was about to plunge. I had been responsible for Trinity's Botanic Garden at one stage of my career. I was familiar with the restoration and conservation of Trinity's historic buildings and had some experience of planning procedures. Perhaps most importantly, I was used to working with the public service on conservation issues and thought that help might become available. In brief, the role matched my earlier experience very well. After reflection for a month or so, I agreed that I would be willing to become Chairman.

Of my new colleagues on the Trust, Tom Raftery, the Secretary, was Professor of Agriculture at UCC and was at various times a Senator and a Member of the European Parliament. His energy and commitment have been critical to the progress of the Fota project. Without him there would have been no future for the Trust. I admire his work greatly and we have become very good friends. Aidan Brady had been acting as Chairman when I arrived, but serious medical problems led to his death after a few short years in 1993. Cormac Foley of Dúchas had responsibility for several botanic gardens in State care in the south-west. He replaced Aidan on the Trust and gradually took over the management of Fota's Gardens. David Bird, a farmer from near Cobh was, with myself, without an institutional affiliation. He had chaired the Queenstown Project and was well respected in conservation circles. He succeeded me as Chairman in 2001. In addition, members of Cork County and City Councils, including the County and City Managers, attended regularly and were an important source of strength, both psychologically and financially. Kevin Mulcahy, manager of Fota Golf Club attended and proved a helpful neighbour.

Fota Island in Cork Harbour is fringed by the road from Cork to Cobh and is joined to the mainland by bridges. The Island's 500 acres had formed one estate, the property of the Smith-Barry family whose ancestry can be traced back to mediaeval times to a Barry from south Wales, a 12th century Norman invader. John Smith-Barry enlarged the House, which had originally been used as a hunting lodge, in the 1820s. The architects were Richard Morrison and his son William. The Estate had held together much later than many other 'Big Houses' many of which had been destroyed in the 'Troubles' of the 1920s or whose owners had sold up and left Ireland. Its late survival meant that some who worked in the house and gardens are still living and many grandparents or parents of the present generation knew it as a working estate.

James Hugh Smith-Barry, John's son, began the Arboretum, the collection of trees which is the heart of the Gardens, but it was his young son Arthur Hugh who developed the Gardens to their present splendour. Arthur Hugh was ennobled as Baron Barrymore in 1902, dying in 1925. His younger daughter Dorothy (Mrs Bell) inherited the Estate and managed it until her death in 1975 when it was sold to University College, Cork. The intention was that it would be used by the College for training and research in farm management and dairy science. The Smith-Barry family continue at residences in Gloucestershire and Cheshire.

The initial UCC interest in Fota wilted under relentless criticism of its management and bad publicity in the media. The College withdrew and the Estate was sold to property developers. By then some 100 acres had already been allocated to a Wildlife Park linked to the Dublin Zoo. It has been very successful with up to 300,000 visitors in 2003. In 1983 the College had permitted Richard Wood, a prominent Cork businessman, to use Fota House as a centre to display his collection of Irish landscape paintings together with appropriate furniture, carpeting and curtains. Its splendid appearance at that time is well recorded in a booklet, 'Fota House' in the Irish Heritage Series. It was also described by John Cornforth in *Country Life* (1986). The House received the European Museum of the Year Award in 1984. In its peak years the House attracted 15,000 visitors.

The management model followed was broadly that of a major National Trust house in Britain, displayed as a house in use. Richard was personally wealthy and put a great deal of time and energy into the House and Gardens at Fota. Unfortunately, several things went wrong. A collapse left a hole in the roof of the large drawing-room, the room with the most ornate plaster work and the most beautifully decorated ceiling in the House. The House had to be closed to visitors because of safety and insurance concerns. The future of the House and Gardens had become uncertain.

A succession of representatives of the property developers who had acquired the property from UCC now appeared, first the London and Edinburgh Trust (LET), then Firago plc. They were primarily interested in investment in leisure activities, especially a golf-course and also time-sharing apartments with possible development for luxury housing and a hotel. Time-sharing in the region proved to be a declining interest, but the final owners, Fota Ireland Golf Club, have developed a first-class golf course which hosted the Murphy's Irish Open in 2001 and 2002. The original farm buildings of the Estate, which were distant from the House, were skilfully adapted to make a fine club-house and restaurant. The golf course occupies some 300 acres of Fota Island.

The developers did not see a role for themselves in the House, Gardens and some additional farmland, about 115 acres in all. They disarmed potential public criticism by establishing that this should become a 'heritage area' under the control of an independent charitable trust. The initiative to create a trust came from LET prompted by the local authority and must be admired as essentially altruistic. This was the origin of Fota Trust which, treading where angels might have worried, assumed responsibility for the House and Gardens. The scene when I became Chairman in 1991 was a closed House with problems of leaky roofs and dry-rot, neglected gardens with a small staff still paid by UCC and some farm land, leased annually for grazing cattle. We also had a modest income from parking fees, shared with the Wildlife Park, and from grants of £25,000 annually from each of the two local authorities, Cork City and County Councils.

Our first task was to complete the drafting of Articles of Association so that the Trust had legal status as a tax-exempt charity with a governing Board. Early on we gave priority to the Gardens with considerable uncertainty as to whether we would ever be able to tackle the problems of the House. We were much relieved when the State agency Dúchas (now, as far as Fota is concerned, re-absorbed into the Office of Public Works) took over responsibility for the gardeners' wages and, in due course, we arrived at a legal agreement by which Dúchas would manage the gardens as our agents.

We had also received valuable advice on managing the gardens from Dr David Robinson, a distinguished horticulturist recently retired from the Institute of Agriculture. In a few years paths were cleared, fallen trees removed and an extensive programme of planting had begun. In spite of criticism about tree-felling, some trees in the Gardens were near the end of their natural lives and had to be replaced. In one severe storm on Christmas Eve 1997, a dozen or more large mature beeches and Spanish chestnuts came down and took months to clear because of a shortage locally of heavy equipment to move the amount and weight of timber involved. On the day following the storm a huge cedar of Lebanon fell. Its roots were probably disturbed by the powerful wind of the previous day. It was the oldest recorded planting (1824) in the Arboretum, which still contains many splendid specimen trees.

The Orangery in the gardens, now magnificently restored, but at first roofless, was approached by a path between two tall Canary Islands palms (*Phoenix canariensis*). One was simply smashed and beheaded in a later storm. Two young successors have been planted which will replace the older generation in due course. The storms show the necessity to develop and extend shelter belts around the periphery of the Gardens which need protection from salt spray from Cork Harbour and possible pollution from industrial development which is uncomfortably close. Until now wind damage during storms has been of greatest concern.

There are several walled gardens at Fota, one newly planted with choice climbing plants, a collection of Irish-bred daffodil varieties, a great diversity of roses and many others. In 1991 it had simply been ploughed up and manured. The so-called Italian Garden has a fine collection of herbs and has shrubby climbers on a sunny wall. There is a wonderful abundance of butterflies late in Summer. The Italian Garden is now restored. The addition of decorative statuary for some of the original statuary which has been lost is anticipated. Dúchas has been determined that the Gardens should be restored to their late 19th century appearance as far as is possible but some innovation and new plants can, of course, be considered.

Early on we sought the advice of the Office of Public Works on the restoration and conservation of the House. It was helpful that it had earlier been given a high priority for conservation by the Heritage Council, proof of the value of recording conservation priorities even when action was much delayed. We were pleased at the interest expressed by the OPW and subsequently we received, and continued to receive, invaluable help. At first our income permitted only minor capital works. We re-roofed buildings in the Stable Yard near the House and extended our work to re-roofing the servants' quarters in a wing of the House which had become rather derelict.

Our builder, Paddy O'Donovan, was a very reliable helper. He also restored gates and buttressed walls which had begun to lean in the walled gardens. John Cahill of the OPW advised us on the standard of work to be sought and on the reasonableness of cost estimates. It may be unusual to record the work of the Civil Service whose good deeds tend to be clouded in secrecy, but John's magnificent skill and untiring commitment deserve every praise. We held out for high quality workmanship at all times. One phrase of Michael O'Doherty, Principal Architect in the OPW, stuck in our minds. We should 'protect the envelope' of the House, in other words give absolute priority to stopping rainwater leaks, to repairing window frames and roof damage so as to stabilise the House for a full programme of conservation in an unknown future.

One piece of good fortune came our way. In November 1993 the Trust had negotiated a legal agreement with Firago plc, then owners and potential developers of the Fota Estate, to the effect that the costs incurred by the Trust in the management and care of the House and Gardens would be provided for. This had amounted to £20,000 in a typical year. The agreement was, however, open-ended and placed no financial limit or time constraint on the amount of subsidy we could request. This was surprising but with our limited resources and probable lack of legal 'muscle' it seemed unlikely that we could spend large and ever-increasing sums of money without a legal conflict which we would probably lose. I suggested that we could cancel this part of our agreement in return for a once-off capital sum of the order of £300,000. I asked John Mahony, then Chairman of the OPW, an always helpful and wise counsellor, whether this was sensible. 'Do you think you can get it?' was his reply. A sum of £330,000 was agreed with Firago, rather to our surprise, but it set us on the road to more serious work on the House.

Richard Wood's paintings were still hanging in the House, a particularly gloomy prospect in winter when the House was unheated and heavy with condensation. After negotiations of some complexity Richard removed his pictures to the University of Limerick where they are now displayed. His furniture and other fittings were put in store. This was a necessary precondition for a serious look at the condition of the House which involved tearing out damaged floors and walls. Not surprisingly, there was extensive dry-rot and the ceilings needed to be repaired. A very thorough overhaul was undertaken. We were greatly helped by the expertise of the architects of the Office of Public Works, especially John Cahill, who supervised and planned much of the work carried out. We were supported by a Dúchas grant of £500,000. A Bord Fáilte grant of £1.6 million was obtained in 1999 and a special grant of £1 million in the State budget of 2000. We had calculated that the complete restoration of the House would cost £5 million. We still have some way to go, but work on the ground floor is essentially complete. The upper floors still present problems both financial and practical, especially in satisfying fire safety requirements.

At the conclusion of the work of conservation the roof of the House had been fully repaired and the chimneys, one of which leaned alarmingly, had been straightened. The ceilings are now held in place by steel girders and the wonderful plasterwork and painted ceilings restored in exacting detail by specialists. Floors have been replaced where necessary and dry-rot damage removed. There is an automatic temperature and moisture control system so that the gloom and dank of the past should not be repeated. The work is a wonderful memorial to the people who carried it out.

The rest of the story belongs to others. The intensity of work locally as the restoration was completed and the House re-opened made a chairmanship from Dublin unrealistic. I was glad to step down in favour of David Bird after ten years in office. I continue to be a member of Fota Trust and attend business meetings regularly. President Mary McAleese performed the formal opening of the house on April 30th, 2002 with her usual skill and grace. It was a very fine occasion.

The completed physical restoration still leaves problems with providing furnishings of all kinds where there is much still to do. The return of Richard Wood's paintings and furniture to the House was not pursued as a possibility by our under-resourced Trust. The newly formed Irish Heritage Trust would probably favour their return if this can be arranged. The House is open to visitors and used extensively for receptions. There are interactive touch screens in several rooms which describe the House, the Gardens and their history. The historic kitchen is fully restored and stocked with period utensils. It is adjoined by an unusual octagonal game larder. Peter Brears, a specialist in historic kitchens and how meals were prepared, describes it all on a touch-screen.

At present the scheme has been an outstanding success. For the future some questions remain. Should the rooms be largely unfurnished so that their architectural qualities and beautiful decorated plasterwork can be admired or should there be a greater effort to provide furniture which would make the rooms less usable for receptions and public occasions? Would it be more attractive to the visiting public if it had more the character of a museum? The public response is very important because even as many as 15,000 visitors annually is probably not enough to provide a sufficient income base. Admissions to the Gardens must be free in order to accord with Dúchas policy but we still need to pay staff wages and ever-increasing costs of which insurance is a well-known problem. Do we charge enough for receptions or do too many receptions and functions compromise the integrity of the House as a heritage building? Should the State have a larger involvement? 'Probably', is the only possible answer. These headaches are for our successors to struggle with, but they must be resolved for long-term stability and success.

The State had been giving consideration to founding a new National Trust to manage historic houses, partly funded by the State, partly funded from private sources. Fota was mentioned as possibly the first National Trust House. In August 2007, the Irish

Heritage Trust came into existence with Government funding for some of its costs. Ownership of Fota House and Gardens, with all their promise and problems, passed to the new body in January 2008. May they succeed! Thus Fota Trust, a voluntary body, passes into history, rewarded by its success in preserving and protecting a beautiful house and gardens.

Epilogue

17.
RETIREMENT AND AFTERTHOUGHTS

IN MY LAST YEAR AS PROVOST I became ill. Earlier, asthma had been suspected, but John Pritchard, a senior lecturer in cardiology, examined me and dismissed it as a possibility and pointed to a heart problem. If I had been more observant of myself I would have diagnosed a heart problem, but it came to a head in January of 1991 when a day arrived on which I could hardly walk upstairs or even eat anything. I was taken urgently to St James's where I was quickly treated and my condition stabilised, then to the Adelaide under the care of the gentle and considerate Ian Graham. An electrocardiogram showed a very irregular heart beat with a somewhat enlarged heart and weakened heart muscle. I sneaked a look at the medical charts at the foot of my bed which read, 'showed incipient heart failure'. Happily it was halted at the incipient stage and, with appropriate medication and some dieting, I made a good recovery. I still have the same irregular heartbeat with atrial fibrillation, now a permanent feature of my life. I was back at work within a month.

My illness had good and bad aspects. On the good side it made for easy acceptance of my retirement which was statutorily required to take place by the following July 31st. Left with the choice of reverting to a professorship or retiring on a Provost's pension which had financially identical consequences, the latter choice was an easy winner. I advised the Board of my intention to retire and to resume a career of writing and research. Some may have feared that I would seek a second term which is statutorily possible but, apart from the possibility of being rejected by the electorate, ten years in the modern Provostship is so punishing, as my health record showed, that I doubt whether anybody will ever seek a second term. Gerry and I began our move back to our Stillorgan house in May 1991 and began the task of overseeing painting and decorating, tidying up the garden, and other chores.

The College's fourth centenary in 1992 fell shortly after my retirement. The new Provost, Tom Mitchell, had taken up office as August began. He had delegated much responsibility for organising the fourth centenary celebrations to David McConnell, Vice-Provost for the Quatercentenary. I treated myself to field work in Florida while the celebrations took place. I didn't want to tread on Tom's feet or have him feel that he should constantly refer or defer to me. During my Provostship I had organised the construction of the O'Reilly Institute and the Samuel Beckett Theatre to mark the Fourth Centenary. I had insisted on a fireworks display and organised the publication of several books about the history of the College and inventories of its treasures, the sort of useful records that don't get put together at more ordinary times.

The bad part of retirement was, what do I do now? I had thought, but not very productively, of a part-time business career with a non-executive directorship or two. I had been assured that I would be an asset to any business. All this turned out to be fantasy, so I returned happily to a research career, because I had enough money to live a comfortable enough suburban life and money was not my prime motivator.

I became much involved with Fota House and Gardens as I have related and continued my interest with the Mercer's Foundation. With each, after a ten or more year involvement as Chairman, I became a, still active, ordinary member. Five years ago I was appointed Chairman of the Dublin Dental Hospital by Minister for Health and Children, Micheál Martin. Until December 2006 I presided as Chairman over Board meetings and selection committees for senior appointments. The hospital is a large activity with a budget of €22 million, but I was not concerned with the detailed day-to-day management of the Hospital which is managed by a Dean, a Chief Executive and a variety of committees. I enjoyed the work. Soon I will revert to the simpler pleasures of a 77 year old, gardening, reading, modest exercise, lots of pills, as my College career, which has been so much of my life, finally runs its course.

Appendices

Appendix 1
ELECTION TO PROVOST
IN 1981

	First Round	Second Round	Third Round	Fourth Round
C. H. Holland	46	–	–	–
D. I. D. Howie	48	52	–	–
M. Ó Murchú	97	100	120	138
T. D. Spearman	60	76	88	–
W. A. Watts	90	114	136	205

Appendix 2
SCIENTIFIC PUBLICATIONS

This is a list of my most cited publications. Three, marked with asterisks, have over 100 citations. All but two of the others have been cited between fifty and one hundred times. Two with more than 30 citations are of Irish interest which have a limited potential readership outside Ireland. I do not know how this compares with the work of other scientists, some of whom will have been cited very many times. My hope is that it is at least respectable. My total of publications is about 70.

Watts, W.A., 1959, 'Interglacial deposits at Kilbeg and Newtown, Co. Waterford', *Proc. Roy. Irish Acad.*, V. 60B, pp79–134.

Watts, W.A. & Wright, H.E. Jr, 1966, 'Late-Wisconsin pollen and seed analysis from the Nebraska Sandhills', *Ecology*, v.47, pp202–210.

* Watts, W.A. & Winter, T.C., 1966, 'Plant macrofossils from Kirchner March, Minnesota — a paleoecological study', *Geol. Soc. of America Bulletin*, v.77, pp1339–1359.

Watts, W.A. & Bright, R.C., 1968, 'Pollen, seed and mollusk analysis of a sediment core from Pickerel Lake, Day County, South Dakota', *Geol. Soc. of America Bull.*, v.79, pp855–876.

Watts, W.A., 1970, 'The full-glacial vegetation of northwestern Georgia', *Ecology*, v.51, pp17–33.

Watts, W.A., 1973, 'Rates of change and stability in vegetation in the perspective of long periods of time', pp195–206 in Birks, H.J.B. and West, R.G. (eds.) *Quaternary Plant Ecology.* Oxford, Blackwells, 326pp.

Watts, W.A., 1975. 'A late-Quaternary record of vegetation from Lake Annie, South-central Florida', *Geology*, v.3, pp344–346.

Watts, W.A., 1977, 'The Late Devensian Vegetation of Ireland', London, *Royal Soc., Phil. Trans.* B280, pp273–293.

William Watts — a Memoir

* Watts, W.A., 1979. 'Late-Quaternary vegetation of Central Appalachia and the New Jersey coastal plain', *Ecological Monographs*, 49, pp427–469.

Watts, W.A., 1980, 'Regional variation in response to Late-glacial climate events in Europe', in Lowe, J.J., Gray, J.M. and Robinson, J.E. (eds) *Studies in Late-glacial of North-west Europe*. Pergamon Press, London, pp1–22.

Watts, W.A., 1980, 'Late-Quaternary vegetation history at White Pond on the Inner Coastal Plain of South Carolina', *Quaternary Research*, 13, pp187–199.

Watts, W.A., 1980, 'The Late-Quaternary vegetation history of the southeastern United States', *Annual Reviews of Ecology and Systematics*, 11, pp387–409.

Watts, W.A., and Stuiver, M., 1980, 'Late Wisconsin Climate of Northern Florida and the Origin of species-rich Deciduous Forest', *Science*, 210, pp325–327.

Watts, W.A. and Bradbury, J. Platt, 1982, 'Paleoecological Studies at Lake Patzcuaro on the West-Central Mexican Plateau and at Chalco in the Basin of Mexico', *Quaternary Research*, 17, pp56–70.

Watts, W.A., 1983, 'Vegetational history of the Eastern United States 25,000 to 10,000 years ago', in Porter, S.C. (ed.) *Late-Quaternary Environments of the Unites States, Vol. 1. The Late Pleistocene*. University of Minnesota Press, Minneapolis, pp294–310.

Watts, W.A., 1985, 'Quaternary Vegetation Cycles' in Edwards, R. J. and Warren, W.P. (eds.) *The Quaternary History of Ireland*, Academic Press, London.

Watts, W.A., 1985, 'A Long Pollen Record from Laghi De Monticchio, Southern Italy: A Preliminary Account', *Journal of Geological Society*, v.142, pp491–500.

* Grimm, E.C., Jacobson, G.L., Watts, W.A., Hansen, B.C.S., Maasch, K.A., 1993, 'A 50,000-year Record of Climate Oscillations from Florida and its Temporal Correlation with the Heinrich Events', *Science*, 261, pp198–200.

Watts, W.A., Allen, J.R.M., Huntley, B., 1996, 'Vegetation History and Climate of the Last 15,000 years at Laghi di Monticchio, Southern Italy', *Quaternary Science Reviews*, 15, pp113–132.

Watts, W.A., Allen, J.R.M., Huntley, B., 1996, 'Vegetation history and palaeoclimate of the Last Glacial Period at Lago Grande di Monticchio, Southern Italy', *Quaternary Science Reviews*, 15, pp133–153.

Grimm, E.C., Watts, W.A., Jacobson, G.R. Jr, Hansen, B.C.S., Almquist, H.R., Dieffenbacher-Krall, A.C., 2006, 'Evidence for warm wet Heinrich events in Florida', *Quaternary Science Reviews*, 25, pp2197–2211.

Appendix 3
COMMENCEMENTS AT
THE UNIVERSITY OF
DUBLIN IN 1816

William S. Guinness to Benjamin L. Guinness   12th July 1816

My Dear Ben,

I had intended writing to you yesterday in reply to your kind and interesting letter
of the 5th inst, which I received on Tuesday but was prevented by circumstances
from fulfilling my intention. On Tuesday last I took my degree of A.B. and am
consequently henceforth entitled to the appellation of Bachelor of Arts.

The ceremony was somewhat impressive in appearance. Chief Justice Downes[1]
as Vice Chancellor of our University presided on the occasion dressed in his
Judicial robes, and on his left hand sat the Provost in his complete Academic dress.

At each side of the Vice Chancellor and the Provost forming a half circle about
them were arranged the Senior and Junior Fellows, the Masters and Scholars
decorated with their appropriate robes, and all the badges of their respective degrees.

---

[1] William Downes, Lord Chief Justice of Ireland was also Vice-Chancellor of the University and
his full size portrait in full judicial robes hangs in the Dining Hall of the College. The Provost
was Thomas Elrington, whose portrait may be seen in the Common Room. Both portraits and
brief biographies can be found in Crookshank and Webb, number 4 in the Quatercentenary
series (see Bibliography). The Guinness letter is a typescript copy found in family papers by Lady
Normanby (Grania, Dowager Marchioness of Normanby) who gave permission for it to be
published. She presided over Commencements as Pro-Chancellor from 1984 until her retirement
from the post in 1996 and so was well placed to recognise that the letter was an important
record. The original has not been found at present.

In front of the Vice Chancellor and Provost was placed a large Table covered with a green baize cloth, upon which were laid several College papers and old bibles with several other fusty old books. There was also the original copy of the College Statutes in manuscript, which was written in the old English hand upon very coarse parchment. It is about ten inches square, and bound in a most strangely durable manner: the covers and back are of tanned brown leather half an inch thick and straped (*sic*) with brass, studded into the leather. It is a very curious looking article and was written in Queen Elizabeth's reign, since which time it has been preserved with the utmost care. We the Candidate Bachelors knelt at the Table and repeated, after one of the Senior Fellows, who read them out of the Copy of Statutes, certain oaths in the Latin language: the purport of which was, that we observe allegiance to King George, and his descendents who shall inherit the throne of this United Kingdom: that we abjure the legitimacy of the Pretender's (or rather his Descendents) claim to the throne of England Scotland or Ireland and that we would inform of any conspiracies against the King and Government which should come to our knowledge. Then, having previously signed our names in a book, wherein the oath was copied we individually knelt upon a cushion at the V. Chancellor's feet, and having laid our hands upon another velvet cushion upon the table before him, he covered them with his and pronounced in Latin the form of conferring the Degree. We were then dismissed with a short sentence pronounced by one of the Senior Fellows in the Latin Language.

I was disappointed with hearing that the return home was defer'd: but when I consider the reason I feel reconciled to the delay, in hopes that the visit to Lymington may complete the re-establishment of our beloved Mother's health. I am glad you have seen Blenheim: it is by all accounts a munificent testimony of British gratitude and admiration. I suppose you saw the Duke of Wellington before you left Cheltenham: we see by the News papers that he is much followed by public admiration. "tis not surprizing. I should like to see so great a Hero!

I had intended to make this a joint letter to you and Susan, to whom I must soon write a long epistle, by way of atoning for my past taciturnity in epistolary converse. Tell Father (who I trust is now perfectly recovered from his late attack of inflamed eyes) that we have mowed Nos. 7: 7½: 8: 9: 11: and 2: but were obliged to stop last Saturday night, in consequence of the frequent rains, which had impeded the making up of what was mowed previous to that time: Next Monday we shall, please God, recommence at the Mowing. The grey Mare I have been obliged to send to Watts, being very ill with an inflammation of the Lungs, similar but not so violent as what she had about two years ago, when she was also sent to Watts by my Father. She is much recovered now. I have not been successful in my exertions to discover the Plunderers of the School House but as some suspicion rested upon Pilkington and Sutton, and Giltrap wished to get rid of Sutton on account his disobedience to him in various instances, I discharged them both. Tell my Father that Giltrap is quite recovered. Your Greyhound little Camilla is become a very beautiful dog and I have brought her into some obedience but not so amenable as poor Fleet, who is grown a very large and swift hound. Arthur and I have our two ponies at Brookville since the Grey Mare's illness. Tommy is quite a curiosity for his fatness. You might almost as reasonably expect the saddle not to turn if put upon a rolling stone as upon his little carcase. It is (indubitably) time and place for me to conclude being 3 o'clock P.M. and having advanced in cross bar writing to this extremity of my second page: Therefore, My dear Ben, I shall now take leave of my pen for the present, and conclude with affectionate love to my dear Parents, and Sisters and your good self by subscribing myself

Your truly affectionate Brother
Wm. S. Guinness

James Gate.

P.S. Excuse the illegibility of the latter part of this prolix composition, for the point of my pen is Become quite soft from work.

P.P.S. You owe me a long description letter for this epistle.

Historical note, based on *The Guinness Spirit*, Michele Guinness, Hodder & Stoughton, 1999
    The letter seems to be from William Smythe Lee Grattan Guinness (1795–1864) to his brother Benjamin Lee Guinness (1798–1868). William was the eldest son of Arthur Guinness (1768–1855) of St James Gate, who was in turn the son of the founder of the brewery, Arthur Guinness (1723–1803). William became a Church of Ireland clergyman, and Benjamin, later Sir Benjamin, was responsible for the rapid expansion of the brewing business, became Lord Mayor of Dublin and funded the restoration of St Patrick's Cathedral.
    The text is from a typed copy provided by Grania, Marchioness of Normanby, former Pro-Chancellor. The location of the original letter is not known.

Appendix 4
BIBLIOGRAPHY

A selection of further reading, descriptive accounts of the College and its buildings and other matters discussed in the text are given below.

The College — older records
Anon., *The Portfolio of Trinity College, Dublin*, W. H. Beynon & Co., Cheltenham, c. 1920, (contains interesting early photographs of the College, its buildings and their interiors).
Bailey, K. C., 1947, *A History of Trinity College, Dublin, 1892 to 1945*, Dublin.
Mahaffy, J. P., 1904, *The Particular Book of Trinity College, Dublin*. A facsimile from the original, J. Fisher Unwin, London, 258p.
Maxwell, C. 1946, *A History of Trinity College, Dublin, 1591–1892*, Dublin.
Stubbs, J. W., 1889, *The History of the University of Dublin from 1591 to 1800*, 429p, Hodges Figgis & Co., Dublin.

The College — Publications for the Quatercentenary
Trinity College Dublin Quatercentenary Series, published by Trinity College Dublin Press:
No. 1 Bennett, Douglas, 1988, *The Silver Collection Trinity College Dublin* 154p.
No. 2 Scott, David, 1991, *The Modern Art Collection Trinity College Dublin* 101p.
No. 3 *Trinity: One of the Great European Centres of Learning* (An Introductory Pamphlet published by the Board of the College. It contains excellent photographs).
No. 4 Crookshank, Anne and Webb, David, 1990, *Paintings and sculptures in Trinity College, Dublin*, 205p.

211

No. 5 Luce, J. V., 1991, *Orationes Dublinienses Selectae (1971–1990)*, 123p.
No. 6 Holland, Charles (ed.), 1991, *The Idea of a University;* 384p, in particular see McParland, E. J., 'The College Buildings', pp153–184.
No. 7 Luce, J. V., 1992, *Trinity College Dublin: The First 400 years* 246p.
No. 8 Webb, D. A. (compiler), Bartlett, J. R. (ed.) *Trinity College Dublin Record Volume 1991* 170p, the so-called *Red Calendar*.

Scott, David (ed.), 1992, *Treasures of the Mind, a Trinity College Dublin Quatercentenary Exhibition*, 176p, published by Sotheby's London.

The College — other accounts

Crookshank, Anne, 1986, 'The Long Room', pp16–28 in *Treasures of the Library, Trinity College Dublin*, ed. Peter Fox, Royal Irish Academy, Dublin.
Fox, Peter (ed.), 1986, *Treasures of the Library, Trinity College Dublin*, 258p, Royal Irish Academy Dublin.
McBrierty, V. J., 2003, *Ernest Thomas Sinton Walton, the Irish Scientist (1903–1995)*, 98pp, Trinity College Dublin Press.
McDowell, R. B., and Webb, D. A., 1982, *Trinity College Dublin 1592–1952 An Academic History*, 580p, Cambridge University Press.
Scattergood, John, 2006, *Manuscripts and Ghosts, Essays on the Transmission of Medieval and Early Renaissance Literature*, 300p., Four Courts Press Dublin.
Watts, Geraldine, 1988, 'The Provost's House, Trinity College Dublin', pp144–151 of *In an Irish House*, Ed. Sybil Connolly, Weidenfeld and Nicholson, London.
Wyse Jackson, Peter, 1987, *The Story of the Botanic Gardens of Trinity College, Dublin 1687–1987*, Pamphlet published by TCD Botanic Gardens.

Fires in the College

Lamacroft, Jane, 1986, 'Forged in the Fire', *Designer's Journal* 22, 46–50.
Olley, John, 1987, 'Rebuilding in a Classical Tradition', *Architects' Journal*, 185, 37–56.
Reihill, Ann, 1986, 'The Restoration of the Dining Hall, Trinity College Dublin', *Irish Arts Review* 3, 26–37.
Webb, Michael, 1986, 'From the Ashes', *Chartered Quantity Surveyor* 8, 11, 21–23.

Athy

Farren, S., 1995, 'Irish Model Schools 1833–70, Models of what?', *History of Education* 24, 45–60.

Teachers and Mentors

The Liberal Ethic, 1950, The Irish Times, 89p. A vigorous correspondence on the nature of liberalism from *The Irish Times*, January–March 1950.

Watts, W. A., West, R. G, 1999, 'George Francis Mitchell, 15 October 1912 – 25 November 1997', *Biographical Memoirs of Fellows of the Royal Society of London*, 45, pp315–328.

Climate and Quaternary History

Judy R. M. Allen, Ute Brandt, Achim Brauer, Hans-Wolfgang Hubberten, Brian Huntley, Jörg Keller, Michael Kraml, Andreas Mackensen, Jens Mingram, Jörg F. W. Negendank, Norbert R. Nowaczyk, Hedi Oberhänsli, William A. Watts, Sabine Wulf & Bernd Zolitschka, 'Rapid environmental changes in southern Europe during the last glacial period', 1999, *Nature*, 400, letters pp740.

Achim Brauer, Judy R. M. Allen, Jens Mingram, Peter Dulski, Sabine Wulf, and Brian Huntley, 2007, 'Evidence for last interglacial chronology and environmental change from Southern Europe', *Proceedings of the National Academy of Sciences of the United States of America*, 104 No. 2 pp450–455.

Barnosky, A. D., (1985), 'Taphonomy[2] and Herd Structure of the extinct Irish elk', Megaloceros giganteus, *Science*, 228, 340–344.

C. F. G. Delaney and I. R. McAulay, (1959), 'A radiocarbon dating system using scintillation techniques', *Scientific Proceedings of the Royal Dublin Society*, Series A1 pp1–20.

Crises

Hussey, Gemma, 1990, *At the Cutting Edge*, 271p, Gill and Macmillan, Dublin.

Royal Irish Academy

Mitchell, F. J. G, (ed.), 2001, *From Palaeoecology to Conservation: An Interdisciplinary Vision, Biology and Environment*, 101B, pp164, (the Watts 'Festschrift').

Ó Raifeartaigh, T. (ed.), 1985, *The Royal Irish Academy, a Bicentennial History 1785–1985*, p351, Royal Irish Academy, Dublin.

Hospitals

Coakley, Davis., 1992, *Irish Masters of Medicine*, 370p., Town House, Dublin. Contains photographs of Dr Steevens' Hospital and The Worth Library.

Fitzpatrick, D, (ed.), 2006, *The Feds, An Account of the Federated Dublin Voluntary Hospitals 1961–2005*, p330, A. and A. Farmer, Dublin. Contains a paper entitled 'Why did Edward Worth (1678–1733) leave his books to Dr Steevens' Hospital?' by W. J. McCormack, Librarian in charge of the Worth Library.

Lyons, J. B., 1991, *The Quality of Mercer's. The Story of Mercer's Hospital, 1734–1991*, 215p, Glendale Publishing Co., Dublin.

---

[2] Taphonomy is the study of stratigraphic occurrence of fossil bones.

McCarthy, Muriel, 1986, 'An Eighteenth Century Dublin Bibliophile', *Irish Arts Review*, 3(4), 29–33, An account of Dr Edward Worth and his library.

Mitchell, David, 1989, *A Peculiar Place, The Adelaide Hospital 1839–1989*, 336p, The Blackwater Press, Dublin.

Conservation

An Taisce, 1967, *Study of Amenity Planning Issues in Dublin and Dun Laoghaire*, 54p, Brunswick Press, Dublin. (No named author, but Kevin Fox was a major contributor.)

Bond, Valerie, 2005, *An Taisce — The First Fifty Years*, 255p, The Hannon Press, Ballivor, Co. Meath.

McDonald, Frank, 1985, *The Destruction of Dublin*, 346p, Gill and MacMillan, Dublin. Contains references to An Taisce's contribution to planning issues.

Quirke, Bill, E. 2001, *Killarney National Park, a place to treasure*, 234p, the Collins Press, Cork. A fine evocation of the Park with unusual information and photographs.

Fota

Bowe, Patrick, 2005, 'Fota Gardens — Island Oasis', *Irish Arts Review*, 22/1, 114–119. The modern Fota Gardens restored.

Butler, Patricia, 2004, *Treasured Times, A memory of Fota House 1947–1975*, 77p, Recorded by Eileen Cronin and published by Fota Trust Limited. Patty Butler was variously housemaid, cook and housekeeper in Fota House in its last days as a private 'Big House'.

Wood, Richard, 1984, *Fota House*, No. 44 in Irish Heritage Series, 35p, Eason & Son Limited, Dublin. The prize-winning house recorded prior to closure.

Hymans, Edward and McQuitty, William, *Irish Gardens*, 1967, pp76–81, London, McDonald & Co. Gives an account of Fota Gardens and a photograph of the Italian Garden with statuary.

Leland, Mary, 2002, 'Revealing Fota's Glories', *Ireland of the Welcomes*, 50, 32–41. A detailed well-illustrated article with much interesting information.

St Leger, Dr Alicia (Ed.), *Fota House and Gardens*, 2002, 29p, City Print. Pamphlet on the restoration of the House, fully illustrated.

Medical Education and Numbers in Training

Fottrell, Professor Patrick, 2004, *Medical Education in Ireland, a New Direction*, Report to the Higher Education Authority.

INDEX

St Andrew's College, 26
St James's Hospital
  originally St Kevin's, 159
St Patrick's Cathedral, 111
Taisce, An, See An Taisce
Tallaght Hospital Board
  Butler, Michael, 165
  Conroy, Richard, Chairman, 165
  Hurley, Dr Gerry, 165
  Rogan, Desmond, Acting Secretary, 165
Trinity College Dublin
  Apied, Mary, 105
  Arbuthnott, John, 5, 139
  Arnould, EJF, 30
  ban removed 1970, 85
  Beckett, Samuel, 133, 137
  Board, 95, 101, 106
  Boatman, Derrick, 43
  Body Corporate, 100
  Book of Durrow, 141
  Book of Kells, 140, 141
  Botanic Gardens, 45
  Botany (1907) & Physics (1905)
    buildings by FitzGerald and Joly, 64
  Brian Boru Harp, 147
  Burke, Edmund, portrait by James
    Barry 1771, 144
  Bursar, 96
  campus companies, 67
    ERA/MAPTEC
      founded 1986, 67
  Clarke, Aidan, 120
  Clarke, George, 105
  Coakley, Davis, 59, 162
  College Officers, 96
  Corish, Sean, 67
  Coutts, Archie, 29
  Crookshank, Anne, 132
  Cullen, Louis, 124
  d'Estaing, Giscard, 149

Dawson, George, 6, 44, 100
Delaney, Cyril, radiocarbon dating, 70
Dining Hall fire, 125
  Al Byrne film, 126
  de Blacam and Meagher, architects, 126
  Frederick Prince of Wales, portrait by Thomas Hudson, 126
  restoration Cramptons builders, 125
Dixon Hall, 131
Dixon, AF, 131
Dixon, HH, 131
Doherty, Michael, 87
Examination Hall, 5, 107, 113
  restoration, 132
Fabian Society, 29
Farhat, Hormoz, 107
Fellowship, 64
Finance Committee, 104
financial problems of 1980s, 104
Fitzgerald, GF, Erasmus Smith's Professor of Natural and Experimental Philosophy from 1881, 63
Foundation Scholarship, 37
Fox, Peter, 141
Furlong, Edward, 100
Gainsborough, Thomas, painting of John Russell, 144
Gibney, Arthur, architect, 139, 140
Giltrap, Gerry, College Secretary, 102, 103, 120, 125, 127
Glucksman Map Library, 135, 141
Goldsmith, Oliver, Sizar, 29
Guinness, Lady Grania, 55, 139
Haughey, Charles, 7, 110
Hamilton Building, 134
Hamilton, William Rowan, 139
Harvey, WH, 45